Terrism or sp'n –
World politics—20th century
Civil War

Editor: Catherine Bradley
Designer: Charles Matheson
Researcher: Cecilia Weston-Baker

Illustrated by Paul Cooper and Ron
Hayward Associates

© Aladdin Books Ltd 1987

Designed and produced by
Aladdin Books Ltd
70 Old Compton Street
London W1V 5PA

First published in the
United States in 1987 by
Franklin Watts
387 Park Avenue South
New York, NY 10016

ISBN 0-531-10385-4

Library of Congress Catalog
Card Number: 87-50225

Printed in Belgium

Front Cover: Members of the Irish Republican Army give victory salutes in Belfast, 1982.

TERRORISM AND CIVIL STRIFE

CHRIS COKER
Edited by Dr John Pimlott

FRANKLIN WATTS
New York · London · Toronto · Sydney

INTRODUCTION

Pressures on the world community are many and varied. Each particular region – Europe, the Americas, Africa, the Middle East and Asia – has its own problems and causes of conflict. As the number of independent countries in the world has grown, particularly as a result of the European countries giving up their Empires, so the nature and extent of global problems has changed. This volume identifies and analyzes these problems and, wherever possible, outlines potential solutions.

High on the list is the question of inequality, especially in economic terms. As a rough guide, the world may be divided into the "rich" countries of the North and the "poor" countries of the South, producing tension as the former use their wealth and power to impose their own terms of trade. Although this has yet to produce violence on a large scale, the potential for North-South conflict undoubtedly exists and efforts must be made to ensure a more equal distribution of wealth if it is to be avoided. Up to now, these efforts have not enjoyed success.

But violence does come from other sources, notably the small groups of people who, for political or nationalistic reasons, resort to terrorism to achieve their objectives. Hijacks, bomb attacks and indiscriminate killings are a feature of modern life. The nature of terrorism and the problem of making appropriate responses is a major theme of this volume and one which highlights the international rather than the regional tensions of the modern world.

International problems demand international solutions, and the final chapter deals with the United Nations as a potential source of such solutions. The record is not impressive, for the United Nations inevitably reflects the tensions among its members, but the fact that it exists as a forum for debate does offer at least a glimmer of hope for the future. If attempts are not made to solve the problems of the world, they could become overwhelming.

DR JOHN PIMLOTT *Series Editor*

EDITORIAL PANEL

Series Editor:
Dr John Pimlott, Senior Lecturer in the Department of War Studies and International Affairs, RMA Sandhurst U.K.

Editorial Advisory Panel:
Brigadier General James L Collins Jr, US Army Chief of Military History 1970-82

General Sir John Hackett, former Commander-in-Chief of the British Army of the Rhine and Principal of King's College, London U.K.

Ian Hogg, retired Master Gunner of the Artillery, British Army, and editor of *Jane's Infantry Weapons*

John Keegan, former Senior Lecturer in the Department of War Studies and International Affairs, RMA Sandhurst, now Defense Correspondent, *Daily Telegraph*

Professor Laurence Martin, Vice-Chancellor of the University of Newcastle-upon-Tyne U.K.

The author: Christopher Coker is a Lecturer in the Department of International Affairs at the London School of Economics and Political Science. He is the author of *US Military Power in the 1980s, NATO, the Warsaw Pact and Africa*, and *A Nation in Retreat*.

Terrorism and civil strife in Northern Ireland: a burning bus in Belfast, 1981. Since 1969 Northern Ireland has been the scene of unrest and fighting because of the struggle between Loyalists and Republicans. The British Army was sent in to keep the peace and has been under pressure from the Irish Republican Army (IRA), the main organization fighting for a united Ireland. The IRA does not see itself as a terrorist organization, despite its many attacks on public places.

CONTENTS

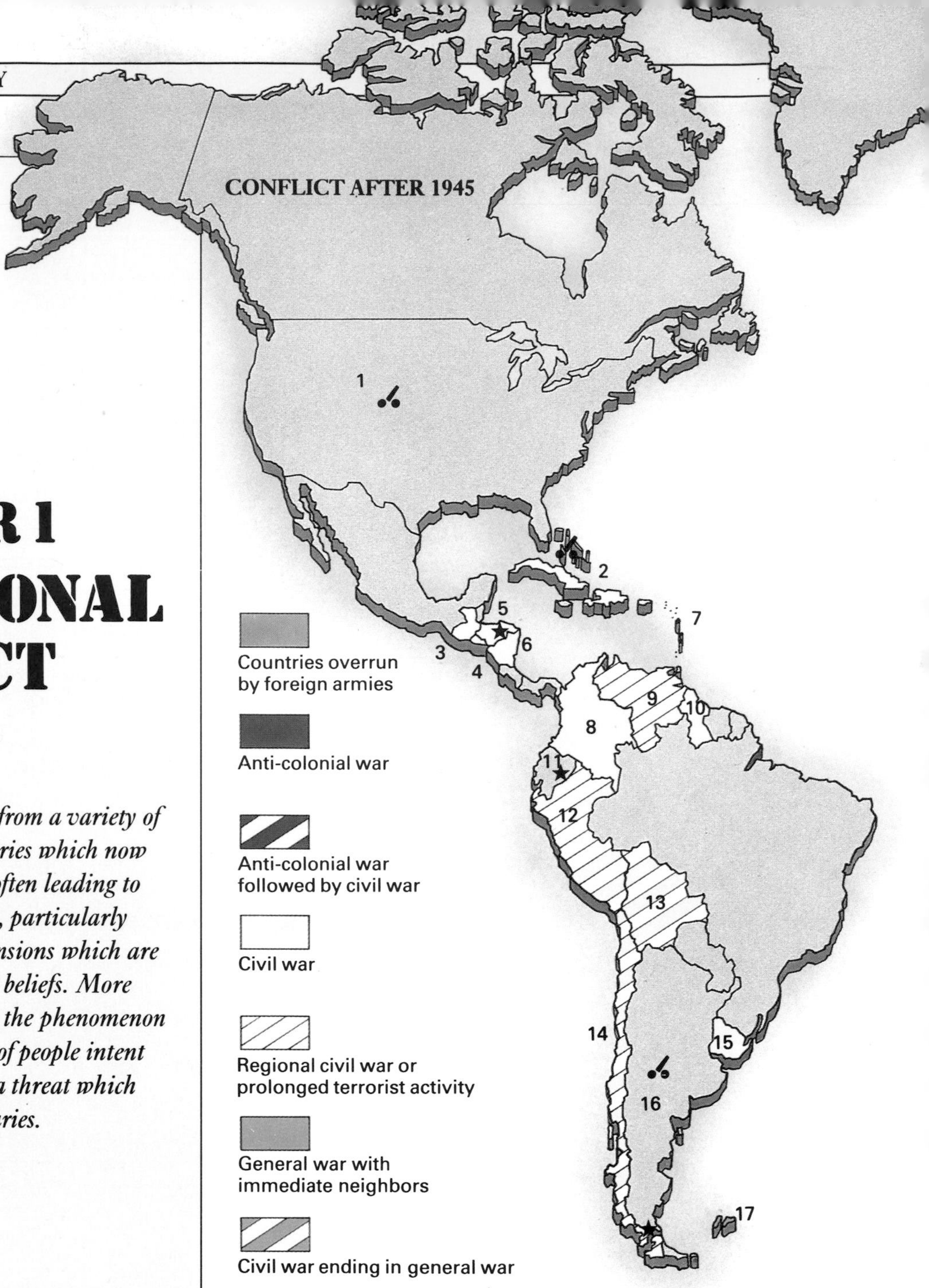

CONFLICT AFTER 1945

CHAPTER 1 INTERNATIONAL CONFLICT

Violence in the modern world stems from a variety of sources. The large number of countries which now exist produce territorial disputes, often leading to war, while economic inequalities, particularly between North and South, create tensions which are often fueled by differing political beliefs. More dramatically, the world is subject to the phenomenon of terrorism, used by small groups of people intent upon political change, producing a threat which ignores national boundaries.

Countries overrun by foreign armies

Anti-colonial war

Anti-colonial war followed by civil war

Civil war

Regional civil war or prolonged terrorist activity

General war with immediate neighbors

Civil war ending in general war

Since the end of the Second World War in 1945, there have been hundreds of military conflicts in the world. Despite the emergence of what the Canadian professor, Marshall McLuhan, once called "the global village," life has not been made safer by the increased speed of travel, the spread of communications, or the extension of trading relations and economic activity. Indeed, quite the reverse is true. Today it may take less time to fly from London to Sydney than it took to travel from London to Scotland 150 years ago, but the world is also a more dangerous place for the many people who live in it.

It is in part because of the shrinking globe, because of the phenomenon of "interdependence" (the extent to which one country depends upon the next, particularly in terms of trade) that conflict is so marked. Years ago people hoped that an interdependent world would make for less strife, not more. In some parts of the world, notably Western Europe where both world wars broke out, this has proved to be the case in the post-1945 period. In the world at large, however, it has not. For example, there have been many civil wars, that is wars between rival groups in the same country. These have occurred in Lebanon, Chad, Nigeria, Angola, Nicaragua, El Salvador and elsewhere.

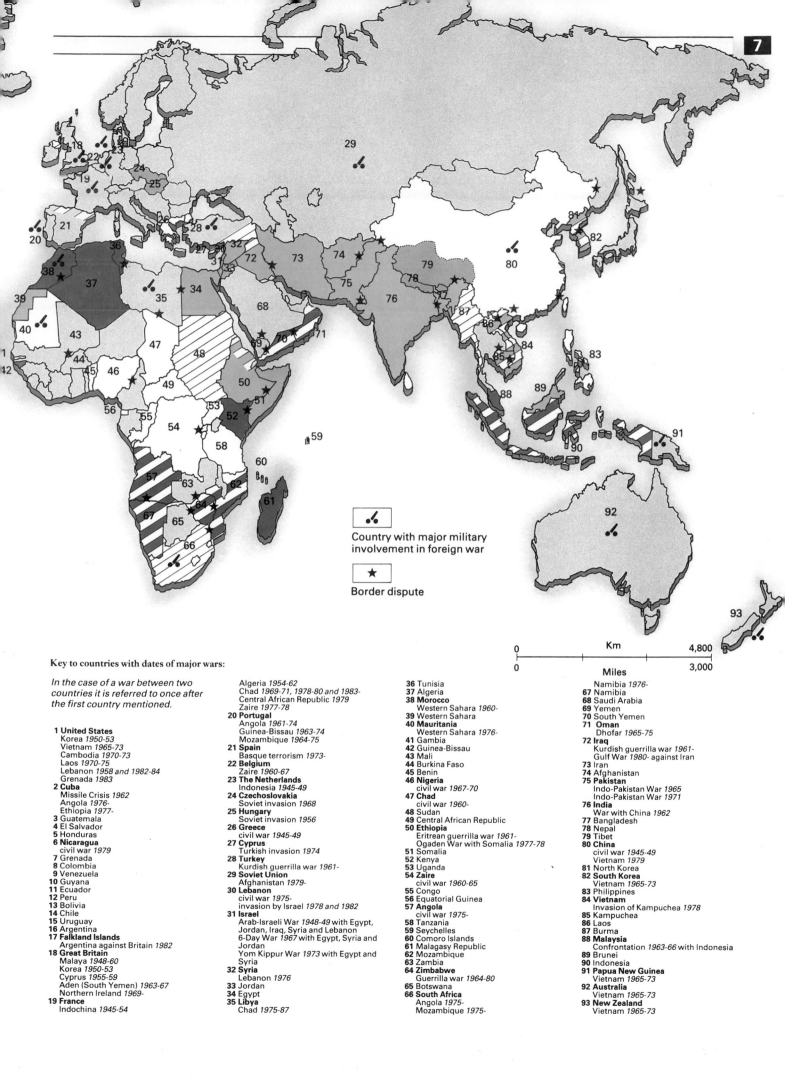

Country with major military involvement in foreign war

★ **Border dispute**

Km
0   4,800

Miles
0   3,000

Key to countries with dates of major wars:

In the case of a war between two countries it is referred to once after the first country mentioned.

1 United States
Korea *1950-53*
Vietnam *1965-73*
Cambodia *1970-73*
Laos *1970-75*
Lebanon *1958 and 1982-84*
Grenada *1983*
2 Cuba
Missile Crisis *1962*
Angola *1976-*
Ethiopia *1977-*
3 Guatemala
4 El Salvador
5 Honduras
6 Nicaragua
civil war *1979*
7 Grenada
8 Colombia
9 Venezuela
10 Guyana
11 Ecuador
12 Peru
13 Bolivia
14 Chile
15 Uruguay
16 Argentina
17 Falkland Islands
Argentina against Britain *1982*
18 Great Britain
Malaya *1948-60*
Korea *1950-53*
Cyprus *1955-59*
Aden (South Yemen) *1963-67*
Northern Ireland *1969-*
19 France
Indochina *1945-54*

Algeria *1954-62*
Chad *1969-71, 1978-80 and 1983-*
Central African Republic *1979*
Zaire *1977-78*
20 Portugal
Angola *1961-74*
Guinea-Bissau *1963-74*
Mozambique *1964-75*
21 Spain
Basque terrorism *1973-*
22 Belgium
Zaire *1960-67*
23 The Netherlands
Indonesia *1945-49*
24 Czechoslovakia
Soviet invasion *1968*
25 Hungary
Soviet invasion *1956*
26 Greece
civil war *1945-49*
27 Cyprus
Turkish invasion *1974*
28 Turkey
Kurdish guerrilla war *1961-*
29 Soviet Union
Afghanistan *1979-*
30 Lebanon
civil war *1975-*
invasion by Israel *1978 and 1982*
31 Israel
Arab-Israeli War *1948-49* with Egypt, Jordan, Iraq, Syria and Lebanon
6-Day War *1967* with Egypt, Syria and Jordan
Yom Kippur War *1973* with Egypt and Syria
32 Syria
Lebanon *1976*
33 Jordan
34 Egypt
35 Libya
Chad *1975-87*

36 Tunisia
37 Algeria
38 Morocco
Western Sahara *1960-*
39 Western Sahara
40 Mauritania
Western Sahara *1976-*
41 Gambia
42 Guinea-Bissau
43 Mali
44 Burkina Faso
45 Benin
46 Nigeria
civil war *1967-70*
47 Chad
civil war *1960-*
48 Sudan
49 Central African Republic
50 Ethiopia
Eritrean guerrilla war *1961-*
Ogaden War with Somalia *1977-78*
51 Somalia
52 Kenya
53 Uganda
54 Zaire
civil war *1960-65*
55 Congo
56 Equatorial Guinea
57 Angola
civil war *1975-*
58 Tanzania
59 Seychelles
60 Comoro Islands
61 Malagasy Republic
62 Mozambique
63 Zambia
64 Zimbabwe
Guerrilla war *1964-80*
65 Botswana
66 South Africa
Angola *1975-*
Mozambique *1975-*

Namibia *1976-*
67 Namibia
68 Saudi Arabia
69 Yemen
70 South Yemen
71 Oman
Dhofar *1965-75*
72 Iraq
Kurdish guerrilla war *1961-*
Gulf War *1980-* against Iran
73 Iran
74 Afghanistan
75 Pakistan
Indo-Pakistan War *1965*
Indo-Pakistan War *1971*
76 India
War with China *1962*
77 Bangladesh
78 Nepal
79 Tibet
80 China
civil war *1945-49*
Vietnam *1979*
81 North Korea
82 South Korea
Vietnam *1965-73*
83 Philippines
84 Vietnam
Invasion of Kampuchea *1978*
85 Kampuchea
86 Laos
87 Burma
88 Malaysia
Confrontation *1963-66* with Indonesia
89 Brunei
90 Indonesia
91 Papua New Guinea
Vietnam *1965-73*
92 Australia
Vietnam *1965-73*
93 New Zealand
Vietnam *1965-73*

Disputed territory

The sources of "international conflict" are many. One of the most common is disputed territory, especially between countries which have only recently become independent. Those countries which were independent in 1945 may have claims against one another, but they are rarely prepared to press them to the point of war.

Most of the countries that were colonies in 1945 have taken a different path, however, calling upon nationalism to reinforce their unity in times of crisis. Sometimes they have encouraged "displaced aggression," a term used to describe how governments deliberately use an external threat, however unreal, to deflect people's attention away from their own political or economic problems. The Argentinian invasion of the Falkland Islands in April 1982, at a time when the military government was under domestic pressure, is a case in point.

Nationalism has for long been a cause of conflict – indeed, one associated with the First World War (1914-18). What makes it such a powerful force in the developing world is that decolonization (the granting of independence to colonies) resulted in an arbitrary division of territory which took remarkably little account of ethnic groups – people sharing a common language, culture or race.

Africa suffered in this respect more than any other part of the world as different tribal groups found themselves trapped in new countries, which had little sense of identity or unity. This led to friction between neighboring countries over territory. For example, Somalia tried to claim the Ogaden region of Ethiopia, because most of its people were nomadic Somalis, who in any case ignored the existence of the Ethiopian-Somali border. This dispute eventually led to a brief but bitter war between the two countries in 1977-78 from which Ethiopia (with Soviet and Cuban aid) emerged victorious.

Refugee problems

When ethnic minorities have not been able to fight for their freedom or call upon the protection of an external power they have often been the victims of ruthless persecution. This, in turn, has led to one of the most distressing international problems of all: that of the mass exodus of refugees or "displaced persons."

Some 250,000 people fled Angola when the civil war started in 1975; 600,000 had left Eritrea (part of Ethiopia) by 1979. By 1970 there were already one million refugees in Africa of whose existence the United Nations was aware. By 1978 that figure had leaped to nearly three million, not to mention a further two million who were officially described as "unsettled" even though they had chosen to return to their country of origin.

The refugee problem is not just a result of international conflict, for in many cases it has actually produced it. The treatment of the Chinese minority in Vietnam contributed to the war between Vietnam and China in 1979, a short but bloody confrontation. The 220,000 refugees who fled from the rampaging Pakistani Army in East Pakistan triggered the last and most decisive of the Indo-Pakistani wars (1971) which saw the birth of Bangladesh.

The Palestinian problem

Elsewhere in the world, the phenomenon of displaced persons has permanently soured relations between countries. Throughout the 1950s the presence of Palestinian refugees in the camps of the Gaza Strip (then part of Egypt) acted as a reminder of the plight of the Palestinian people, a permanent reproach to an Arab world which had failed them in the 1948-49 Arab-Israeli War. Later, when many of them were resettled, more problems were created.

Some of the countries, particularly those which played host to the refugees in the Arabian (Persian) Gulf, adjusted to the change quite easily, even though by the late 1970s those same refugees formed no less than a third of their entire populations. Other societies found them more difficult to absorb, notably Jordan, who found the violent presense of the PLO intolerable and attempted to expel them in 1970. In Lebanon the government's inability to control its Palestinian "guests" provoked two Israeli invasions (1978 and 1982).

Ideology

Ideology, or differing political ideas, has also proved to be one of the most divisive forces of modern times. The Americans, Soviets and Chinese, for example, all became involved in the civil war in Laos between 1959 and 1962, supporting rival groups in their bid for power. Communist governments have continually tried to overthrow non-communist regimes; Western governments have tried to prevent communist movements from coming to power.

This, of course, is nothing new. As long ago as the 1820s Britain, France and Russia intervened on behalf of the rebellious Greeks against the Turkish occupying power. Indeed, the British government was partly spurred on by pressure at home resulting from a campaign led by the poet Lord Byron: one of the first occasions on which events in one country had an impact on people's consciousness in another. In France, popular agitation in 1860 forced the government of the day to intervene on behalf of the Maronite Christians in Lebanon.

Human rights

But in the 19th century the European powers were essentially in agreement about which values they wished to encourage in foreign countries. However, they often chose to ignore the plight of peoples nearer home, whether they were Irish or Polish. No such agreement on values exists today between the superpowers (the United States and Soviet Union) even though both are signatories to the United Nations Declaration on Human Rights. This document was drawn up in 1948 to set a "common standard of achievement for all peoples and all nations" on such issues as political freedom, stateless persons, slavery and discrimination against women.

The problem of different ideas about human rights remains. The West has been accused of being largely indifferent to the problems of hunger and economic want, while, it is argued, the communist states have largely eradicated unemployment and inflation and produced welfare for all, even at the cost of the denial of some fundamental political rights. At the same time, the Eastern bloc has been accused of turning a blind eye not only to the denial of civil rights at home but also some of the crimes carried out in the name of international communism, such as those committed in Kampuchea (previously known as Cambodia).

For three years (1975-79) the Soviet bloc remained largely silent as the Kampuchean government, under Pol Pot, tried to bring about in a matter of months many of the social changes that it had taken Mao's China 25 years to achieve. As a result, the human cost was appalling as political opponents were "psychologically reconstructed," those of middle-class origin murdered, the hospitals emptied of patients, and three million people forcibly moved to the countryside. By the time the government collapsed in 1979, it was estimated that several million people had been killed.

The sprawl of a refugeee camp in the Gaza Strip. In 1985 there were over 200,000 people still living in camps in that area. Some families have lived in refugee camps for two generations.

Some 120,000 Turks live in West Berlin in West Germany. Parts of Kreuzberg have become a Turkish ghetto.

East/West rivalry

In the propaganda war between the superpowers these issues have created a permanent climate of mistrust and misunderstanding. Television and the written word have helped to bring home such violations of human rights as the crushing of the independent trade union movement, Solidarity, in Poland (1981).

For their part, the citizens of the Soviet Union have been shown pictures of the unemployed in the West, images of an apparently uncaring society which has reduced many of its citizens to a poverty-stricken, marginal group. It is not altogether surprising that both East and West feel they have a moral duty, as well as a strategic interest, to extend their influence in the world. They want to export their values, if necessary by force, and to sustain governments which claim to represent them, whether in Afghanistan, El Salvador or anywhere else in the world.

Developing countries

In many of the countries which have gained independence since 1945, little attention has been paid to the question of human rights. For most of the developing nations, collective rights, or the rights of the community, are far more important than individual ones. Economic development is far more central to their interests than the introduction of elections and political choice. Ever since they gained their independence they have continued to call for such basic "rights" as the redistribution of global wealth, calls which were given added weight by the Brandt Commission in 1980 (see below, Chapter 2).

The world debt crisis

Indeed, it is their continuing economic plight which poses perhaps the most serious potential source of conflict in the modern world. The West has tried to tackle some of the most persistent causes of economic conflict such as currency instability – when the value of money on the international market goes up and down – and protectionism – protecting home industries by imposing taxes or tariffs on imports from abroad.

It has tried to do this by creating institutions like the International Monetary Fund and the World Bank, but they have not been able to meet the developing world's needs or aspirations. Tariff barriers continue to prevent the developing world from expanding; most developing countries feel a sense of injustice.

In recent years the Western world has begun to express concern that developing countries may one day use the power of the weak; they may refuse to pay a debt or else restrict the supply of raw materials in order to gain greater advantage in the terms of trade. In the West the threat of a "resource war" is a much discussed possibility.

Foreign workers

Just as the world's political divisions have created the phenomenon of displaced persons, so its economic inequalities have produced a new pattern of human migration – people in search of employment. In some areas of the world, notably Western Europe, the process has its origins in the distant past, in the years before the First World War when Germany absorbed 800,000 workers from Poland every year, and France 40,000 Italians. Since 1945 this pattern has contributed to a process of economic integration which has helped to remove tariff barriers and social divisions and given rise to a unique experiment in political and economic cooperation: the European Economic Community (usually known as the EEC).

Elsewhere, however, the process has produced conflict and social tension. In the small Gulf state of Qatar, for example, 88 per cent of the work force is made up of foreign workers; 53 per cent in Kuwait (the great majority of them Palestinians). In West Africa, Nigeria has absorbed 900,000 workers from neighboring countries. In times of economic prosperity such migrations can be absorbed. In times of unemployment and recession, however, popular pressure means that governments are often forced to expel foreign workers, as Nigeria did in 1985.

Interdependence can break down barriers but it can also create them. For the most part, countries themselves remain minor actors in a greater historical drama over which they have no control and very little understanding.

Liberation wars and terrorism

The third and perhaps the most intractable source of conflict in the modern world is the threat posed by non-government groups, either national liberation movements fighting for independence and freedom, or terrorist movements trying to destroy their own society by attacking the hated symbols of "state oppression."

In the past, such conflicts were largely fought within national boundaries. Today, many are conducted almost exclusively abroad, mostly through acts of terrorism which are intended to win publicity for causes which have long gone unremarked or forgotten. Some of these struggles, like the Palestinian conflict, are already 40 years old; others, like the Armenian attacks on Turkish targets in Western Europe, are even older, a historical reprisal for the massacre of hundreds of thousands of Armenian people between 1895 and 1915.

Justifying the use of force

Inevitably, as civil wars have been fought abroad, innocent people have been caught in the crossfire as the recent spate of hijackings and bombings has shown. The use of force by terrorists represents one of the most serious threats to international order. Governments justify their use of force as a means of last resort. Terrorists tend to use it instead as a means of first resort. This is why terrorism as a political instrument has been condemned by nearly every government in the world, even those strongly in sympathy with terrorist motives. Even so, with events such as the hijacking of the ship *Achille Lauro* (October 1985), the spate of bombings in Paris and the aircraft hijacking to Karachi (September 1986) fresh in peoples' minds, terrorism has clearly become a fact of life on the international scene.

Yet one of the most disturbing trends of recent years has been the tendency of some countries to resort to terrorism themselves to remove political opponents. The global village, as the more far-sighted exponents of world revolution have been preaching since the time of Lev Trotsky, has made it easy for supporters of revolutionary movements to travel.

The governments of Libya, Iran and Iraq are known to have carried out political assassinations against their opponents in the United Kingdom, Italy and France. Reportedly, 10 Libyan exiles were "executed" in Rome, Bonn and London between March and June 1980 on the orders of Colonel Muammar Gaddafi. Western Europe has become a battlefield for rival ideologies and conflicting beliefs, the price that has been paid for shrinking frontiers.

Such, in short, are some of the causes of conflict in the world, many of them differing in importance and scope from country to country. In the chapters that follow we shall discuss in greater detail some of the economic and political implications of interstate tension and violence within states, before going on to look at the main institution for dealing with international conflict: the United Nations.

A shantytown in Mexico City.

CHAPTER 2
THE NORTH-SOUTH DIVIDE

The world is full of inequalities, not least in terms of trade and wealth. The countries of the North, with their money and established power, compete for the mineral resources to be found in the countries of the South but which, in many cases, cannot be exploited without Northern expertise or money. Some Southern countries have tried to band together to change the balance of economic power: whenever they succeed, the potential for conflict will increase.

The world is divided into a number of "sovereign (independent) states" (169 in 1987), each of which occupies a distinct geographical area. Within this area, whose borders are generally recognized by other states, people live under the rule of a particular form of government. The states' leaders theoretically enjoy "the authority of the final word," introducing laws and exercising power (the ability to influence the actions of others). They take action in an effort to achieve maximum benefits for their state.

The interaction of states on the world stage, each pursuing different aims of foreign policy, creates what is known as the International Political System. Each state tries to achieve what its leaders feel is essential for survival – keeping its territory intact, national wealth, access to markets and protection from potential enemies. The state's leader pursues these aims using a mixture of diplomacy (persuading other states to accept its needs), economic power and force. Because some states are more powerful than others, either through size, economic strength or geographical position, the system is inherently unequal and constantly fraught with danger.

First, Second and Third World

In an effort to reflect the reality of the international system, it has become normal to divide states into different categories, based upon their strength and influence. The most common such division, introduced in the 1950s, is the idea of the First, Second and Third Worlds, largely based on political considerations.

Thus, the countries of the First World (Western Europe, North America, Australasia and Japan) comprise those which pursue the ideals of parliamentary democracy, accepting the need for public debate and regular elections to a central governing body. By comparison, the Second World (essentially the Soviet Bloc and China), prefers the ideals of communism, with its belief in strong government free from the pressures of opposition. This is the basis for the main ideological split in the modern world – that between "West" (First World) and "East" (Second World).

This leaves the majority of countries, situated in Latin America, the Middle East, Africa and Southeast Asia, to be lumped together into the Third World, characterized by its general lack of power and influence. This stems from the fact that the countries involved are, in most cases, struggling to develop the political and economic structures so essential to stability. For this reason, they are often called "developing states" and some commentators even distinguish a group within them, known as the Fourth World, which remains much weaker than the rest.

An inadequate framework

All this is unsatisfactory on a number of counts. First, not all countries fit neatly into the categories laid down. In Western Europe, for example, some states have adopted political systems which are far removed from the principles of democracy – Greece, for example, was ruled by a military "junta" between 1967 and 1974. In the Second World, differing interpretations of communism, particularly by the Soviet and Chinese communist parties, do not make for common interests. Second, many states, particularly in the Third World, regard the use of such terms as insulting, implying as they do that First World states have somehow achieved a superior form of government which other states have to struggle to match. Finally, and perhaps most importantly, the division is not very accurate, ignoring the power and influence of some Third World states (notably those with access to oil, principally in the Middle East) and presuming that the East-West divide is the only important element in international politics.

North and South

This latter point has led, in more recent years, to an acceptance that the world can be divided far more realistically into "North" and "South." Although exceptions will inevitably still exist, such a division, based on economic rather than political considerations, offers a more dramatic and immediate view of the problems of the world.

To put it in very general terms, those countries which occupy the Northern Hemisphere – Europe (both East and West), North America and Japan – are richer, more stable and less prone to natural disasters such as floods, earthquakes or droughts than those of the Southern Hemisphere. Obviously, countries such as South Africa, Australia and New Zealand do not fit the pattern, while poverty and natural disasters are by no means a monopoly of the Southern states, but as a rough-and-ready guide to the world, this North-South divide has much to commend it.

By concentrating on economic and social differences, a greater understanding of world problems can be gained. This is particularly the case when it is realized that the states of the North enjoy advantages of wealth, industrialization and stability which many of those of the South can only envy. This leads to friction as the South demands a more equal distribution of resources and power. However the North, conscious of its need to maintain the living standards of its people, continues to resist these demands and ignores this very real problem. It is perhaps the most fundamental cause of latent conflict in the world today.

The South's problems

Unfortunately, in its 30-year existence as a separate entity, dating from the beginning of European withdrawal from its Empires, the South has been able to do little to create the changes it desires. Between them , its member states may encompass a large enough part of the world to form a potentially powerful voice, but they are inhabited by people with little economic strength. Canada, for example, with a population of 24 million, has more industrial power than the whole of black Africa, whose population is 15 times larger.

Nor is this caused purely by lack of development or economic growth in the Southern countries. Many have, in fact, grown wealthier, only to face the problem of rapidly growing populations. Unfortunately, in some societies, despite development, the actual proportion of the total population living in absolute poverty appears to have increased.

Relieving poverty

The precise nature of mass poverty, and the appropriate means of relieving it, seems to differ from country to country. Some rapid-growth economies such as Taiwan have reduced poverty and income inequality in the course of the last decade; other rapid-growth countries such as Brazil have reduced the proportion of absolute poor but have increased the gap between the richest and poorest members of the population. At the same time, some countries, such as Sri Lanka, which have experienced slow economic growth, have managed to reduce absolute poverty while remaining comparatively poor; in others, such as India, the number of people below the poverty line has increased substantially despite great strides towards industrial self-sufficiency by the government.

India, in fact, illustrates the dilemma which so many Southern countries face. Even if the poorest 60 per cent of its population were to receive 40 per cent of all available income, their average annual wage would remain less than $100 per person. The solution, in other words, cannot be limited to a fairer distribution of existing resources; more wealth must be created. The problem is that obstacles to wealth creation exist both within and between the countries of North and South.

The teeming city of Calcutta, India.

Pressures within

At the time of decolonization, political activity in most Southern countries was largely confined to nationalist elites. They were the politically conscious, mainly middle-class members of society to whom the colonial authorities transferred power in the hope that their aims and aspirations would not differ too radically from their own. In terms of lifestyles and attitudes, many of these elites have remained highly Westernized, distant from the majority of their people.

Nevertheless, in their original struggle against colonial rule, many of these elites found themselves having to mobilize large numbers of people in mass demonstrations and strikes, people who had never before been involved in political action. This meant a significant transformation of political life.

Unlike the colonial powers, the governments which replaced them have had to provide a wide range of services to their supporters, including full employment, housing and education. However, they have found themselves increasingly hardpressed to satisfy such basic expectations.

As early as 1971-74 the amounts of money available to governments decreased in every state in Africa, every country in Asia except Japan and every country in Latin America except oil-rich Venezuela. That was before the oil price increases of the mid-1970s, which substantially increased the cost of imported energy for most countries and further reduced the size of government revenue.

Undeveloping countries

Today seven out of ten African countries are poorer in real terms than they were prior to independence. Far from developing, they are actually "undeveloping," a source of grave social and political instability which has given rise to persistent military coups, riots and even insurrections as the people demand services which their governments cannot afford to provide.

In terms of public spending, the gravest problem for the future may well be that of housing; the rapid drift of people to the towns has led to a growth of squatter settlements. Their population is growing at a rate of 12 per cent a year – double the population growth rate of the fastest growing urban centers. The problem of urban slums, of sprawling shantytowns in Latin America and India or the black townships in South Africa such as Crossroads (Cape Town), are those of shortages, excessive crowding and the spread of contagious diseases resulting from inadequate housing.

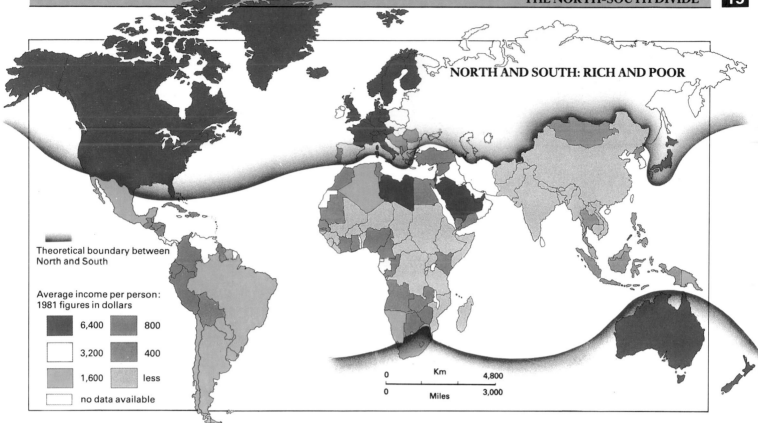

NORTH AND SOUTH: RICH AND POOR

Theoretical boundary between
North and South

Average income per person:
1981 figures in dollars

6,400		800	
3,200		400	
1,600		less	
no data available			

Km 0 — 4,800
Miles 0 — 3,000

Health and social welfare

Health, in fact, is another intractable problem with which most Southern governments have yet to come to terms. The most reliable measure of health available is life expectancy. In the 1980s, people in the North had a life expectancy of just over 71 years. In Africa and Asia, life expectancy was estimated to be about 49 years.

If this were not bad enough, the growing demand for higher spending on social welfare has been resisted by many Southern leaders, such as President Mobutu Sese Seko in Zaire, who has channeled huge sums of foreign aid into private bank accounts in Zurich. Their reluctance to spend more stems from the support they receive from privileged groups in society – from landowners, the army and local business. In some societies (but not all) these groups want to maintain low government expenditure.

Even if more money were to be spent, the political system itself would not be transformed. So far, throughout most of the developing world, political participation, such as it is, has largely taken the form of public demonstrations or riots of the kind which brought down the government of President Ferdinand Marcos in the Philippines in 1986. When governments have agreed to make reforms, these have often been found wanting.

This helps to explain why many Southern societies

are inherently unstable, even violent, and why other forms of civil unrest, from urban terrorism to guerrilla warfare, have become a familiar feature of 20th century politics. Violence is often the only way that the world's poor and dispossessed can find a voice.

North-South tensions

As if this were not serious enough, the Western world has become increasingly aware of the extent to which violence might one day overspill national boundaries and end in conflict between North and South.

What are the South's complaints? To begin with, it believes that the terms of international trade work against it. Foreign investment in a single sector of an economy has made many Southern countries especially vulnerable to falling prices. One such case is that of Oman, whose entire income is derived from the sale of oil.

States which depend on agricultural exports find themselves in an even more precarious position. Not only do they face the threat of bad harvests but also that their traditional markets, especially in the North, might close. To add to their predicament, many developing countries have been forced to produce food for export to earn foreign revenue without being able to feed their own people adequately. Colombia had a substantial surplus on its food trade in the 1970s, yet the food available per head of population remained low.

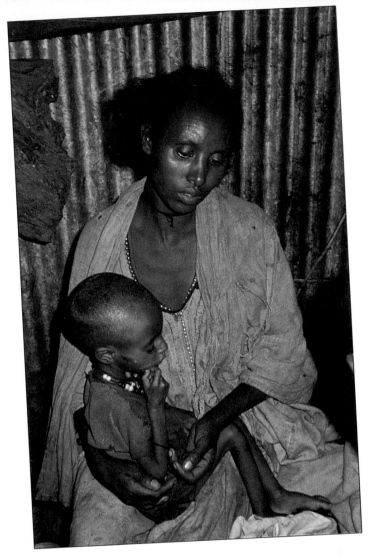

A relief camp in Ethiopia.

Famine in Africa

The case of Africa is more ironic still. Before the famine of 1983-86, the continent had a large food surplus, yet it remained the most undernourished region in the world. In large parts of Africa, government agricultural policies, patterns of land ownership and population pressure have intensified the destruction of land, especially on the edges of the Sahara desert. The prospect of mass starvation presents the Northern world with one of its principal concerns.

In 1977 the United Nations concluded that, with more than a third of all land in the world already arid, well over 600 million people might be affected by the drop in agricultural production by the end of the century, if not before. An earlier United Nations report (in 1974) discovered that, although the proportion of the world population suffering from malnutrition had actually declined, the number of hungry persons had quite certainly increased.

Aid

Furthermore, the economic assistance which the South has received from the North, far from solving its problems, has in some cases merely contributed to them. Foreign aid may not be very substantial in terms of government receipts, but it is often highly significant in terms of government development programs. In many African countries, aid represents 20 per cent of all government expenditure. Between 1960 and 1965 40 per cent of government spending in Pakistan was financed by foreign assistance.

Unfortunately, aid often carries heavy interest payments, especially when loans are provided by the International Monetary Fund (IMF) or the world's leading (Western) banks. As a result, the developing countries have become increasingly indebted. By the mid-1980s, they owed a total of over $300 billion. The international economic order is becoming increasingly unstable. Many states are finding it impossible to live within strained means, let alone develop their economies. In some cases, countries need to borrow simply to repay the interest on their loans.

At the end of the 1970s the most indebted country in the world, Mauritania, owed more than 115 per cent of its annual income. The Sudan owed 80 per cent; Tanzania and Indonesia more than 60 per cent.

Population growth

Perhaps more worrying still is the prospect of population growth. Out of 146 governments surveyed by the United Nations in 1979, no less than 112 expressed the opinion that the rate of population increase was either "substantially unacceptable" or "extremely unacceptable." Only 80 had any policies directed at slowing down (rather than reversing) the trend. Sixteen had no policies at all.

Yet in spite of these grim statistics, there seems to be no immediate prospect of the nightmare world predicted by some futurologists: a world of growing pressure on resources, growth of cities with up to 30 million inhabitants and universal starvation in Southern areas. Instead, it is more likely that population growth will slow down, reflecting a growing realization of its effects and an awareness among the people of developing countries that what little benefits exist cannot be shared out indefinitely.

Indeed, population growth rate had already slowed down from 2.1 per cent during the 1960s to 1.9 per cent in the 1980s. The only exception has been Africa, which is precisely what the experts predicted.

Debt crisis and trade wars

Given such problems, there is the possibility that the South might one day simply refuse to repay what it owes. This would have catastrophic consequences if carried out since it would destroy confidence in the Western banking system (which organizes the loans) overnight and with it confidence in Western manufacturing industry, which also relies on bank loans and available credit to develop.

Only a few countries in the developing world, of course, owe enough to provoke such an impact. Most of them, including Brazil and Argentina, are too closely associated with the Western world to act collectively with more radical anti-Western states.

A trade embargo is also unlikely to happen. In trading terms most Southern countries count for very little. As a trading partner, the whole of Africa is less significant than the United Kingdom; the whole of Latin America less powerful than the Netherlands. It is because the poor countries are marginal to international trade that they have remained marginal powers; as long as they remain marginal they are more than likely to remain poor.

People in India lining up for contraception devices.

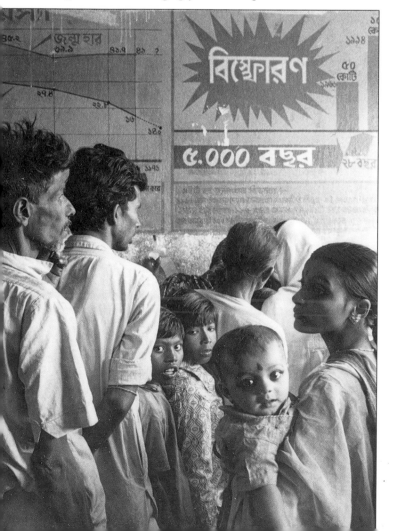

Resource wars

Far more worrying, for Western states in particular, is that in a world of diminishing resources, they seem to be increasingly vulnerable to any interruption in the supply of fuel or non-fuel minerals. Were such an interruption to occur, it might produce havoc in the Western industries.

It is quite possible that the producing countries might attempt to use their control over the production and pricing of raw materials as a means of exerting influence. In the 1990s, nevertheless, the scope for such bargaining is likely to be strictly limited. Indeed, it is possible to identify these limitations by looking at the record of the world's first (and so far only) embargo: that of oil in 1973-74.

The OPEC embargo

OPEC (the Organization of Petroleum Exporting Countries) and its Arab subgroup OAPEC (the Organization of Arab Petroleum Exporting Countries) remain by far the most important coalitions of Southern states to have emerged in recent years. In the early 1970s OPEC was concerned primarily with boosting the income of its own members; OAPEC, geographically centered on the Middle East but holding by far the larger share of the world's oil reserves, with changing the relationship between the West and Israel. In order to achieve both objectives, they had to withhold supplies from their traditional customers without setting back their own economic development.

Their major asset was oil, a commodity upon which the industrial world depended for its most important source of energy. Worldwide demand for oil sharply increased after 1960 as all the European economies as well as that of Japan began to experience unprecedented and simultaneous economic growth which sharply increased their demand for energy imports. At the same time the production of oil in the United States reached a peak and then fell, which made it impossible for it to supply both itself and its allies: Western Europe, Japan, Australia and other countries.

To make the most of these changes, the governments of the producing countries had to gain control over the refining and distribution of oil. A number of the more radical countries, notably Algeria and Libya, led the way by renegotiating their contracts with the world's leading oil companies. Simultaneously, the oil producers gained sufficient reserves of money to enable them to hold out during the time it would take to persuade their customers to pay more.

Raising the oil price

In the event, the 1973-74 embargo, triggered by an Arab desire to counter Western support for Israel, especially during and immediately after the Arab-Israeli War of October 1973, provided a measure of success. On the open market the price of oil quickly rose from $3 to $16 a barrel. Not surprisingly, such "spot" prices persuaded the governments of Algeria and Iran that substantially higher prices could be demanded and maintained if the producers stood together. Under Iranian prodding, an OPEC meeting in January 1974 set a new price for Arabian oil at $11.65, four times what it had been four months earlier.

The actions of the oil coalition sharply changed the flow of economic resources across the world. The foreign earnings of the producers quintupled in less than a year. Saudi Arabia's annual income jumped from $5 billion to $20 billion; Iran's from $4 billion to $17 billion.

European countries, dependent for nearly all their petroleum on the Middle East, were far more severely affected than the United States. Yet the unique combination of circumstances that made the OPEC embargo possible are unlikely to be repeated.

Other possible embargos

Countries producing bauxite and phosphate – Surinam, Jamaica and Guyana – have raised their prices substantially since 1973 and tightened up the conditions under which foreign mining companies can operate. However, they cannot suspend exports for long since they have almost no financial reserves. They depend on the income from exports to sustain the already precarious standard of living of their own people.

The world's copper producers have also tried to act together, only to find that they have little control over price fluctuations, which can wipe out earnings overnight. Demand for copper is far more elastic than demand for oil. In recent years, falling prices have severely damaged such major producers as Zambia. The suppliers of tin had an international Tin Agreement which guaranteed a level below which prices could not fall. But in 1986 overproduction caused the price of tin to collapse, with many countries, for example, Great Britain and Chile, having to close down their tin mines.

For these and other reasons the West probably has little to fear from another OPEC-style embargo. That does not mean, unfortunately, that it has nothing to fear from events in the Arab world.

Temporary stability

Looking back at the 1973-74 embargo, it is surprising how little real damage the West incurred. After the initial shock, the oil-buying countries set up an International Energy Agency to deal with such crises in the future, as well as emergency strategic stockpiles of their own. For their part some of the OPEC states, principally Saudi Arabia, came to depend on a measure of price stability. "Petrodollars" (the money raised from oil) were recycled from the very beginning, with the Saudis earning almost $20 billion a year from their investments in the West. The existence of such capital reserves was to be of considerable strategic importance because it made many Arab governments interested in the continued economic well-being of the North.

Unfortunately, two unexpected developments in 1979 considerably complicated an already complex picture. The fall of the Shah of Iran and the Soviet invasion of Afghanistan raised new questions about the security of oil supply which had not had to be answered in 1974. The fall of the monarchy in Iran posed the question of what might happen to world supplies if a radical anti-Western regime seized power in, say, Kuwait or Saudi Arabia. The Soviet "threat" to the oil-producing areas of the Middle East was also extremely important.

Oil reserves

But how real is the threat? What is the strategic importance of the Middle East and how vulnerable would the Western powers be to another embargo?

To take the last question first, many countries now have sufficient oil reserves to cushion themselves against a short-term loss of oil. At the same time, over-production has led to an oil glut and to a reduction in oil prices. The United States has finally begun to make some progress in building up its Strategic Petroleum Reserve, although it is far short of the eventual target of a billion barrels.

Building up stocks, nevertheless, cannot reduce the West's long-term dependence on Persian Gulf oil; no Western nation could cope with a major reduction in imported oil for more than six or nine months at a time.

Indeed, the industrial countries are almost as dependent as they were 15 years ago. Efforts to increase nuclear power, synthetic fuel and even coal have fallen far short of target. According to one projection, the major industrial powers may fall well below 50 per cent of their 1975 projections of increases in alternative energy sources by 1990.

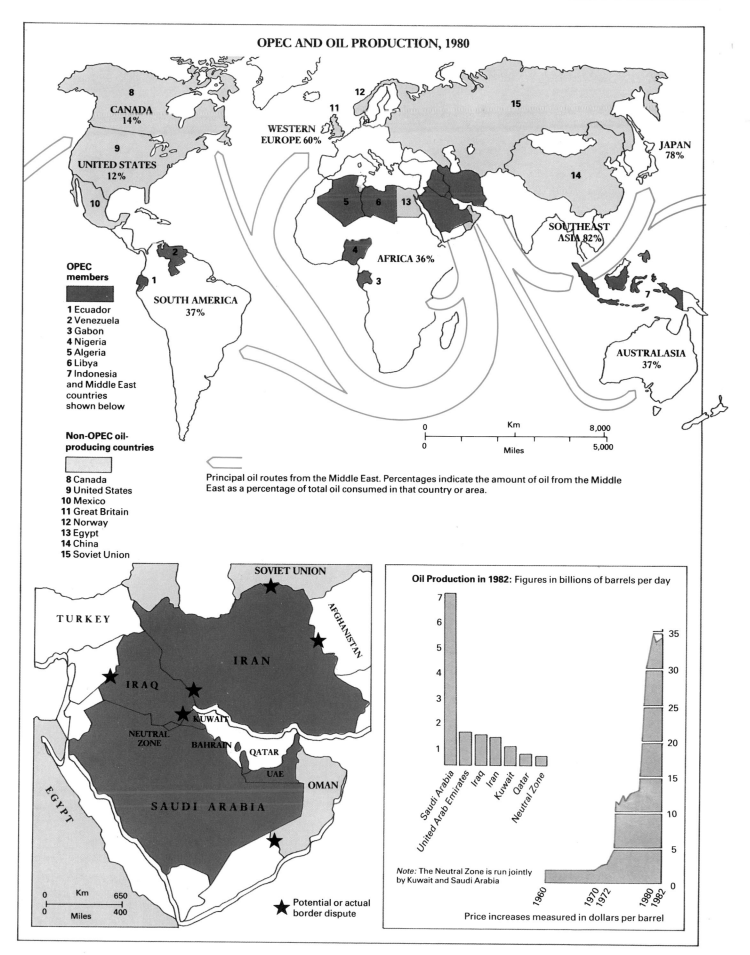

OPEC AND OIL PRODUCTION, 1980

CANADA 14%

WESTERN EUROPE 60%

UNITED STATES 12%

JAPAN 78%

SOUTHEAST ASIA 82%

AFRICA 36%

SOUTH AMERICA 37%

AUSTRALASIA 37%

OPEC members

1 Ecuador
2 Venezuela
3 Gabon
4 Nigeria
5 Algeria
6 Libya
7 Indonesia
and Middle East
countries
shown below

Non-OPEC oil-producing countries

8 Canada
9 United States
10 Mexico
11 Great Britain
12 Norway
13 Egypt
14 China
15 Soviet Union

Km 0 — 8,000
Miles 0 — 5,000

Principal oil routes from the Middle East. Percentages indicate the amount of oil from the Middle East as a percentage of total oil consumed in that country or area.

SOVIET UNION

TURKEY

AFGHANISTAN

IRAN

IRAQ

KUWAIT

NEUTRAL ZONE

BAHRAIN

QATAR

UAE

OMAN

EGYPT

SAUDI ARABIA

Km 0 — 650
Miles 0 — 400

★ Potential or actual border dispute

Oil Production in 1982: Figures in billions of barrels per day

Saudi Arabia
United Arab Emirates
Iraq
Iran
Kuwait
Qatar
Neutral Zone

Note: The Neutral Zone is run jointly by Kuwait and Saudi Arabia

1960 1970 1972 1980 1982

Price increases measured in dollars per barrel

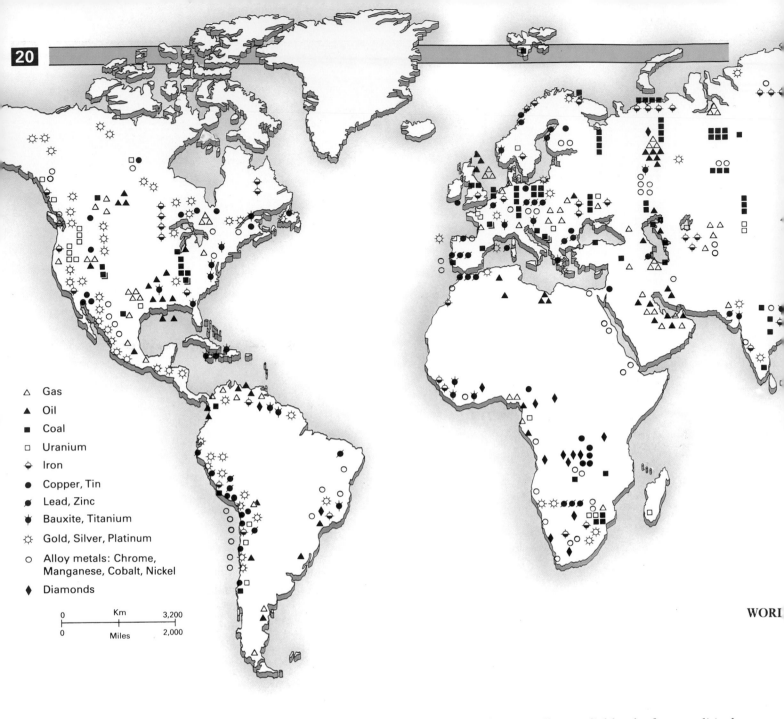

△ Gas
▲ Oil
■ Coal
□ Uranium
⬗ Iron
● Copper, Tin
◓ Lead, Zinc
✦ Bauxite, Titanium
✧ Gold, Silver, Platinum
○ Alloy metals: Chrome, Manganese, Cobalt, Nickel
◆ Diamonds

Km 3,200
0
0 Miles 2,000

WORI

The Gulf's importance

There is also reason to be skeptical about the West's capacity to reduce its dependence on Gulf oil much more than it has already. At present, non-OPEC production is running at 36 million barrels a day. Unless vast new deposits are found in the coming decade, almost all oil production outside the Middle East (in the Soviet Union, Mexico, Alaska and the North Sea) will begin to decline. Consequently any increase in supply will have to come from the OPEC countries. The Gulf's share of total OPEC production will probably rise to 90 per cent by the year 2000 compared with less than 50 per cent in 1973.

Of course, this situation should not necessarily occasion alarm. The record of predictions in the energy field, like the record of predicting political change in the Gulf, has been totally unreliable. As far as political events are concerned, no one in 1973 could possibly have predicted that there might be an embargo, a revolution in Iran, war between two of the Gulf's principal suppliers, Iran and Iraq, or the invasion of Afghanistan, Iran's neighbor.

It could be argued that if the world has succeeded in absorbing this level of instability, things cannot get worse. This may indeed be the case, but it should not be forgotten that in the process the price of oil rose from $2 to $28 a barrel which twice plunged the Western world into recession, first in 1974, and then with the trebling of oil prices between 1979 and 1981. Supply disruptions may not be caused intentionally by the Soviets or militant Arab regimes but their impact on prices may be significant, even profound.

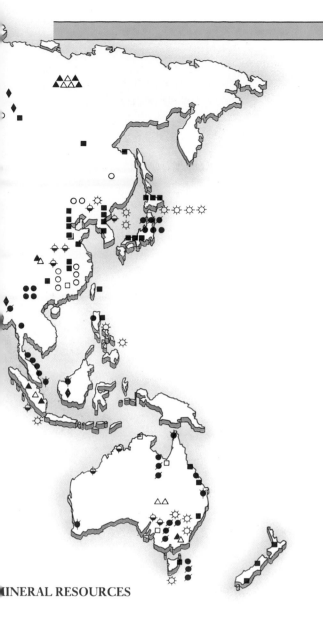

MINERAL RESOURCES

Africa, a region from which they import large supplies of cobalt, chromium and copper, as well as more than 70 other minerals.

We should not leap to the immediate conclusion, of course, that every mineral is "strategically" important, or that its immediate or long term cut-off would be economically disastrous. Strategic importance differs from mineral to mineral and even the industry concerned. In the aerospace industry, for example, it is possible to rank the relative importance of such metals as cobalt (which is used to make gas turbine blades), manganese and copper (which makes the alloys for the main airframes). We can only determine whether one mineral is more or less important than another if we have a clear understanding of what each is used for.

The second industrial revolution
What we do know is that the Western economies have become more dependent on mineral imports in recent years as a result of the "second industrial revolution." High technology industries, for example, require a growing amount of special steels and alloys. Cobalt is essential for computers. The space shuttle program uses twenty critical minerals, most of which have to be imported.

Southern Africa is not the only source of such imports, but the reserves elsewhere are either limited, inaccessible or beyond modern technology, such as the vast but as yet untapped manganese and cobalt "nodules" on the seabed. Deep-sea mining is still only in its infancy.

Declining production
In the United States, domestic production has also declined because it is no longer cost effective. Fourteen of Arizona's 25 copper mines were closed by 1983 because they were no longer internationally competitive. Arizona used to produce two-thirds of America's copper, but is now working at only 60 per cent capacity, with half the industry's work force unemployed since 1981. It is now cheaper to import copper at 65 cents a pound (half a kilo) than to pay an additional 20 cents for home production.

Environmental pressures and the wish to conserve the country's national parks have also forced the closure of all but one plant that is capable of processing chrome. In these circumstances it is not surprising that the United States has expressed serious concern about its dependence on imported minerals, especially from the most important region of all, southern Africa.

In 1979 a four per cent reduction in oil supplies caused by the unrest in Iran led to a price increase of 170 per cent. Even allowing for increased production elsewhere, a complete interruption of supplies today would still create an annual shortfall of something like 10 per cent of present-day demand, which is a much higher percentage than 1973. In other words, the threat should be taken seriously. A conflict in the Middle East still remains one of the greatest single political challenges the West would face short of nuclear war.

Mineral power
The Middle East, of course, is not the only region of the world in which the Western powers appear to face the threat of a resource war. In recent years they have become very concerned about events in southern

Black gold miners in Elsburg, South Africa. South Africa is the largest exporter of gold to the West.

Disrupting supplies

Whether the Soviet threat to southern Africa is any more real than it is in the Gulf, political instability is certainly apparent. Indeed, there have been at least three occasions already in which the West has faced the prospect of interrupted supply of minerals.

During the Angolan civil war in 1975-76 the temporary closure of the Benguela railway, which carries nearly 50 per cent of Zaire's mineral exports to the coast, appeared to threaten the closure of several mines in the province of Shaba (formerly Katanga). In the event, only the copper-mining works at Tenke Fungusume were forced to close down. The others remained open.

Only a few months later, as the war in Rhodesia entered a new and more bitter phase, concern began to be expressed that the fighting would soon extend to the country's chromium mines. Had the war forced mining engineers to abandon operations, the mines on the Grand Dyke might have flooded within six months, those at Selukwe within two. In the four years which it would have taken to reopen them, 25 per cent of the world's production of chromium might have been permanently lost.

More dramatically, events did actually conspire to reduce supplies when rebel forces invaded and brought cobalt production to a complete standstill in the mining town of Kolwezi, Zaire. In the immediate aftermath of the invasion (in 1978) the government was able to operate the mines at only a quarter of their previous capacity. Prices jumped from $6 a pound (half a kilo) to nearly $50. US consumption of chromium from all sources fell by six per cent.

Such evidence suggests that political instability might have devastating consequences. However, most of these African countries rely heavily on exports to finance economic growth. In Zambia the mining sector accounts for no less than 55 per cent of government revenue and 90 per cent of export earnings. Even South Africa, despite its industrial base (the largest in Africa), still relies on mineral exports for 25 per cent of its income, which makes up almost three-quarters of its foreign exchange.

There remains a very real danger, however, that political instability might discourage mining companies from reinvesting their profits or might even persuade them to pull out altogether. This is not a speculative threat, but a real one, for the continent as a whole has been a declining mineral producer for the past 15 years. Of 100 mining schemes that were under consideration in 1970, only seven have been taken up. Fear of political instability has depressed investor confidence. Were South Africa to suffer similar instability, the West might face a very serious threat.

Nuclear threat?

In desperation, the Third World might turn to quite another strategy altogether, resorting to military means rather than economic action.

The threat is not one of conventional war – fought between armies, navies and air forces with non-nuclear weapons. The Northern countries may export arms to the South but the military balance has not shifted in the latter's favor. In 1982 each superpower spent more on its armed forces than the combined national income of the 62 poorest countries in the world. Every year the rich nations spend on development aid less than 0.5 per cent of worldwide military spending.

The danger most talked about is not a conventional war, therefore, but the threat that some 22 countries theoretically could produce nuclear weapons. The fear is not that the weapons would be used but that they would be developed to give the South a louder voice at the conference table. As the African writer, Ali Mazrui, argues, going nuclear would represent a "reassertion of adulthood" which would guarantee if nothing else that the Southern World would at last be given a fair hearing.

Whether or not this argument should be taken seriously, a number of Southern countries have refused to sign the Nuclear Non-Proliferation Treaty of 1968 including India, Pakistan, Brazil and Argentina. But under the terms of the treaty some 120 countries have promised not to build nuclear weapons.

Why go nuclear?

Yet despite the talk, the important fact is that proliferation has not occurred. In the early 1960s it was calculated that 12 countries might go nuclear by 1966. Some 20 years have elapsed and the prediction has not come true. The main reason, perhaps, is that most Southern countries would have remarkably little to gain by becoming nuclear powers.

In the first place the same considerations which influenced the superpowers are likely to influence the lesser states, especially as the countries with the capacity to go nuclear have enemies much nearer home than the Northern countries. Egypt, for example, might like to develop the bomb, since it is now confirmed that Israel has already done so. However, their respective weapons would be targeted against one another. Given that a quarter of the Egyptian population lives in only four cities, Egypt has several targets extremely vulnerable to nuclear attack. This makes it unlikely that she would actually use her nuclear bombs.

Even if some of the more radical, militantly anti-Western leaders might like to engage in a holy war or *jihad* against the West, notably Gaddafi in Libya or the Ayatollah Khomeini in Iran, they would find that, once they had developed nuclear weapons, they could not contemplate war even against their neighbors. Like the superpowers, they would find themselves mutually deterred and forced to accept peaceful coexistence, the uneasy compromise that all nuclear powers have thus far been forced to accept.

Meanwhile, however, the more developed states, especially those of the West (which because of their control of the main instruments of wealth, are held to blame for the present situation by the Southern states) can expect that the anti-Western rhetoric or talk will continue, as too will the threats of direct action if they fail to respond to the South's demands. In fact a reason for not developing the bomb is that if its threats were to cease, the South's only real weapon – its political rhetoric – might lose its impact.

The Brandt reports

This is important because attempts by the international community to tackle the problems of the South have so far failed to make much headway, chiefly because it has proved impossible to agree on a workable solution to such problems. In 1980, the Brandt Commission, chaired by a former chancellor of West Germany, Willy Brandt, presented its "Report on International Development Issues" (subsequently printed under the title *North-South: A Program for Survival*) to the United Nations, only to find that many of its recommendations, including one for the establishment of a world development fund financed by international taxation, were ignored or blocked.

Such reluctance on the part of the West (the only countries with financial means to provide relief) to concentrate resources on the problems of the developing world may be politically understandable, but it does nothing to provide solutions. Indeed, when the starving people of Ethiopia in 1985-86 had to depend upon the efforts of Bob Geldof and Live Aid for relief, receiving aid and development grants from public charity rather than government action, it was obvious that a depressing lack of cooperation existed in the world order. As long as that persists and a basic understanding of the problems of the South remains absent, the pressures caused by poverty, population growth, resource rivalry and natural disasters are likely to increase. It is not a pleasant thought.

A bomb attack in Paris, 1986.

CHAPTER 3
TERRORISM

One of the most worrying developments of the modern age has been the willingness of a country's political opponents to resort to the tactics of terror. Exploiting the advantages which arise from the growth of international travel and communications, they often attack innocent victims, particularly in the liberal democracies of the West, in an effort to force political change. The response of threatened countries has enjoyed some success, but the problem remains.

The use of terror as a political instrument – as a way of "persuading" people to support a particular point of view – is not new. Throughout history, if governments or individuals found that they could not gain support by reasoned argument, violence was always an alternative option, inducing fear in the minds of its victims and forcing them to accept new ideas. Nor should this be surprising: the use of terror is often very easy, and the results are usually immediate, particularly if fear spreads rapidly through an affected society.

Terrorist groups

During the last 20 years the threat of terrorism has grown dramatically. There are a number of reasons why this has happened. First, the period since the late 1960s has seen a vast proliferation of terrorist groups, embracing a wide variety of political and ideological beliefs. In very general terms, terrorist groups have emerged from three distinct sources: from the nationalist demands of ethnic minorities or dispossessed peoples, from the revolutionary activities of predominantly Marxist groups and from the so-called "New Left."

The nationalists, covering groups such as the Palestine Liberation Organization (PLO), Irish Republican Army (IRA) and *Euskadi Ta Askatasun* (ETA Basques), have used terror for some time as part of their campaigns to achieve political recognition and the right of self-government; the IRA, for example, recognized the potential advantages of inducing fear among members of the British security forces (especially the police) during their campaign of 1919-21.

By comparison, the revolutionaries were often forced to adopt terror when their preferred tactics of rural-based guerrilla warfare failed in the mid-1960s. They saw the use of fear as a means of undermining government authority to force change within a state. This happened in Latin America, when the memory of Fidel Castro's success in Cuba (in 1959) was fresh and government responses in the countryside were strong.

Finally, as a separate phenomenon, "New Left" groups such as the West German Baader-Meinhof Gang, the British Angry Brigade, the French *Action Directe* and the Italian Red Brigades, evolved out of the student protests of the late 1960s determined to destroy existing political structures, creating a waste-land out of which new ideas would emerge. The latter were different in that they did not seek political power for themselves (instead, they saw themselves as the "sacrifices" essential for creating the mood for change within society), but they still fitted the general pattern of using terror to force "revolution."

Cooperation between groups

The second reason for the spread of terrorism lies in the nature of our interdependent world, for one of the most worrying factors in recent years has been the way that different groups have cooperated, pooling their resources and using the advantages of modern society to extend their attacks worldwide. A few commentators see such cooperation as part of a Marxist plot to weaken the "Free World" prior to general revolution or invasion, but the reality is probably less dramatic.

Many of the groups, particularly of the "New Left," are small and short of the essentials of a terror campaign – appropriate training, money, arms and explosives – while others, particularly the long-established nationalist organizations, are large, experienced and rich. Among the latter may be included the PLO, organized as a "government-in-exile," with ready access to money from Arab states, training facilities in refugee camps and equipment easily purchased on the world markets.

Members of ETA pose during a training session in the foothills of the Pyrenees.

The connection between the two was natural, especially when, in the early 1970s, Israeli counteractions undermined the ability of the Palestinians to approach their chosen targets inside Israel or among the countries which supported the Jewish state. It did not take much for Palestinian leaders such as Yasser Arafat or George Habash to realize that by offering training, arms and money to smaller terrorist groups, they could recruit men and women who were willing to carry out attacks "by proxy." This would confuse the "enemy" and renew terrorist pressure.

Joint actions

This became apparent as early as May 1972, when three members of the Japanese Red Army (a "New Left" group) attacked the Israeli airport at Lod with automatic rifles and grenades. In fact the majority of people killed were Puerto Rican pilgrims on a visit to the Holy Land, but it soon became apparent that the attack was part of the Palestinian campaign to weaken Israel by persuading people not to visit the country.

Thereafter, links between the PLO and other groups, including nationalists such as the IRA or ETA as well as "New Left" organizations like the Baader-Meinhof Gang (members of which helped the Palestinians to hijack an Air France jet to Entebbe in Uganda in June 1976), became a regular feature of the terrorist threat. Eventually such links were severed by the Israeli invasion of southern Lebanon in June 1982, but a pattern of cooperation had been laid down. Indeed, the Palestinians had even gone so far, in the mid-1970s, as to recruit a coordinator – Ilyich Ramirez Sanchez (popularly known as "Carlos"), a Venezuelan Marxist – to act as contact-man with other groups.

The rising level of terrorist activity since the late 1960s is graphically illustrated by a single statistic: of the 25,181 terrorist incidents recorded since 1968, nearly 83 per cent have occurred in the seven years since 1980. This increase has been due to the fact that terrorists now help each other, but more significantly to the effects of international publicity. Television and newspaper coverage has enabled terrorist ideas to travel from country to country as easily as the terrorists are able to do themselves. In the United States, the Black Panthers produced the White Panthers, while the Tupamaros in Uruguay inspired the creation of "Tupamaros West Berlin."

Not only have the groups helped and inspired each other, they have also copied the methods of other organizations. The hijacking of aircraft was a regular

The official photograph of "Carlos."

ocurrence within the Soviet Bloc until the late 1950s. In the early 1960s it began in the West, reaching a peak of 82 incidents in 1969 alone. The kidnapping of the US ambassador in Brazil, Charles Burke Elbrick, in September 1969 was copied by many groups around the world when it succeeded in effecting the release of convicted terrorists from Brazilian jails. Between then and 1975 there was an attempted kidnapping of an American diplomat once every three months and a successful kidnapping once every five.

A vulnerable world

Several characteristics distinguish present-day terrorism from that of the past. To begin with, terrorists have tried to exploit the technological vulnerability of the modern world. It is now very easy for a group or even a single individual to inflict great damage on society at relatively little cost to themselves.

Reservoirs can be poisoned, electricity power grids put out of action, trains carrying nuclear waste derailed. Offshore oil rigs, natural gas pipelines, computers storing government or company records are all examples of targets which are particularly vulnerable to attack. In 1985, terrorists assaulted electrical power generation installations and transmission lines, petroleum and water pipelines and telephone switching/transmission systems 364 times worldwide.

Occasionally, accidents emphasize the vulnerability of modern society. A telephone exchange fire in the spring of 1975 disrupted services to large areas of New York, in some cases for up to a week. Initially all the city's emergency services were completely cut off and chaos followed.

Perhaps the most daunting target in the future will be nuclear power stations, especially those which are no longer operational and have been closed down. It has been estimated that by the end of the century there will be more than 100 such power plants. There will also be hundreds of smaller nuclear installations from research accelerators to fuel enrichment plants whose productive lives may well be at an end. However, every one of them will remain radioactive and a potential source of danger to local communities.

So far, none of the world's major terrorist movements has tried to bring social life to a complete standstill, but it could actually happen. One group which tried to disrupt social life was the Revolutionary Action Movement (RAM), operating in the United States in the early 1970s. At the height of its activity, RAM carried out a series of attacks, from bombing public buildings to scattering nails at the intersections of highways during rush hour traffic. Like many other militant black groups, including the Black Panthers, RAM believed American society to be so vulnerable that it would fall apart under stress.

The phenomenon of terrorism in the modern era has also been assisted by developments in travel and mass communications: television, videos, newspapers and magazines. Terrorists can move on forged passports and visas with comparative ease; their ideas can travel the world more easily still.

The Latin American connection

In recent years, increasing collaboration between groups within European and Latin American countries has caused alarm. The so-called *Junta de Coordinacion* (coordinating council), existed as long ago as the 1970s in an attempt to coordinate operations by Argentine, Uruguayan and Bolivian terrorists. Today Colombian guerrillas work closely with those in Ecuador, while Ecuadorean revolutionaries have provided weapons for Colombian guerrillas. Most recently, Colombian and Peruvian rebels actually pooled their manpower to form a 500-member joint unit active in the southwest of Colombia.

A hijacked Jordanian aircraft burns at Beirut airport, Lebanon, June 1985.

The impact of television

Most alarming of all, perhaps, is that acts of violence are covered by television, thus conveying the terrorists' message to millions worldwide. Television no longer merely reports events, it can be used to further them as well. The modern terrorist is largely a creation of the mass media.

The two technological changes which made the media so important came in the early 1970s: the introduction of the portable lightweight video camera and the battery-powered portable video recorder, both of which helped to create "instant news." At a siege in Brooklyn, New York, in 1972, the police tried to create a news blackout by shutting off electric power to the area. The television companies responded by bringing in portable generators and floodlights which plunged the hostage-takers into shadow, while silhouetting the police marksmen lying in wait. The police learned much about how to deal with the media during that particular siege situation. During the hijacking of a TWA 747 jet in 1985, hijackers at Beirut airport were able to broadcast their demands on the evening news. Television cameras followed the hijacking story even while the captain, John Testrake, was being threatened.

Middle-class terrorism

The phenomenon of modern terrorism has been shaped, in addition, by a number of factors, each a reaction to modern social trends. In Europe and North America, the affluence of the 1950s and 1960s produced a protest against middle-class lifestyles and the rejection of the capitalist (free enterprise) system.

The reason for terrorist attacks on capitalist targets was stated succinctly almost 10 years ago in an Italian Red Brigades' document, which identified utility networks such as transportation, telephones, gas and electricity as "the fragile links tying together a capitalist state." In an attempt to embarrass capitalist governments, terrorists have struck at the economic base of the nation and hence the ability of the government to govern.

Indeed, as the IRA bombing of the Grand Hotel in Brighton, England, in October 1984 showed, governments themselves may well be the target. In that particular case, Prime Minister Margaret Thatcher, staying in a hotel during a Conservative Party conference, was lucky to escape: as it was, four people were killed and 32 injured in an attack, which, if successful, could have paralyzed (albeit momentarily) the British government.

A television interview with a hijacker at Beirut airport, 1985: pilot Testrake is held at gunpoint.

The Baader-Meinhof Gang

Those who joined the Red Brigades in Italy or the Baader-Meinhof Gang in West Germany were for the most part intelligent student radicals from middle-income families. The Baader-Meinhof Gang was a classic example of a group of disenchanted young people from a privileged background. Andreas Baader (1943-77) was the son of a historian; Ulrike Meinhof (1934-76) was the daughter of an art historian and a graduate in philosophy and sociology. Another member of the group, Gudrun Ensslin (1940-77) was a clergyman's daughter and a graduate in philosophy and languages. Trained by the PLO in Jordan, the gang carried out a number of embassy sieges and spectacular kidnappings in the late 1970s. After their capture, Baader and Ensslin committed suicide in prison, aided by their lawyers who smuggled in guns.

Very few such terrorists, in fact, have truly working-class origins despite their claims and aspirations; none of them succeeded in forging a lasting relationship with any mass movement, not even Western Europe's communist parties, which tended to denounce their actions. As their own political isolation increased, they became increasingly more desperate and violent.

Andreas Baader on the run in Paris.

United States groups

Typical of such groups, the Weathermen in the United States tried to bring down the entire capitalist system by directing 4,300 incendiary bombs against banks and private property in the 15 months before April 1970. Another group, "The Volunteers of America," compared the role of the banks with that of the German financiers who had helped Adolf Hitler in his early rise to power in Germany.

A letter from yet another group, "Revolutionary Force 9," accused such corporations as the computer giant IBM and the oil conglomerate Mobil of degrading their own employees and treating them like "slave labor." These ideas carried no political weight and had little mass appeal. They largely fizzled out with the ending of student protest against the Vietnam War in the early 1970s.

Ulrike Meinhof in 1969.

A car bomb has just exploded in the streets of Beirut, 1985. Many civilians have died in such car bomb attacks. They are usually aimed at specific targets, such as the leaders of rival factions or foreign troops.

Nationalism

A more powerful force is that of nationalism. With a few exceptions (such as Northern Ireland) this has also been a largely middle-class phenomenon, reflecting people's fear of being overwhelmed by the centralized, bureaucratic state. This has taken the form of Welsh-language protesters changing English signposts into Welsh and the bombing of public buildings by Quebe-quois separatists in support of an independent French-speaking state in Canada.

Outside the West, nationalism has usually been a popular manifestation of protest; terror has been a tactic which has met with widespread support. Often terrorism is seen as a traditional form of protest against foreign occupation and rule, with the Palestinians fighting for an independent homeland, Kurds fighting against Iranian and Iraqi rule alike, or Sikh zealots wishing to secede (break away) from the republic of India. Their acts have tended to be far more violent than those of most Western groups.

Many of the hijackings of the early 1970s were carried out or inspired by the PLO. More recently the main perpetrators of hijackings have been militant Sikhs, who were responsible for the worst single incident of air piracy in June 1985, when over 347 people lost their lives in a mid-air explosion.

Muslim extremists

Since the late 1970s the international community has had to contend with a new form of terrorism altogether: that of Muslim extremists protesting at the influence of Western ideas in the Middle East. Inspired by the example of the Iranian revolution, partly funded and directed by the Islamic World Revolutionary Council in Tehran, groups such as the "Islamic Holy War" have successfully carried out attacks against targets as far away as US military bases in Spain.

In Lebanon, Shi'ite Muslim extremists have contributed to massive destruction, indulging in a particularly arbitrary form of violence – car bombings in Tyre and Sidon, and in the suburbs of Beirut. The two most devastating truck-bomb attacks were carried out on October 23, 1983 against the command posts of US and French peacekeeping forces in Lebanon. Some 241 US servicemen and 58 French soldiers were killed.

Often these attacks have been carried out by 15-year-old children, whose video-taped messages relayed on television or broadcast on the radio networks reveal a depth of religious fanaticism which many secular Arab governments, not to mention the non-Muslim world, find almost impossible to understand.

The willing sacrifice of such terrorists does have one thing in common with older forms of political violence – a feeling that their deaths are justified by circumstances of repression and exploitation. This was summed up 20 years ago by writer Frantz Fanon. "At the level of individuals," Fanon wrote in the early 1960s, "violence is a cleansing force. It frees the native from his inferiority complex and from his despair and inaction; it makes him fearless and restores his self-respect."

Does terrorism work?

What then has been the success of terrorism in the past 15 years? Although it has claimed perhaps less than 7,000 non-military victims, it seems to have had a much wider impact than those numbers would suggest. In the absence of reliable data, of course, it is impossible to offer an estimate of the economic costs of such violence. What we can say is that the material losses involved in the hijacking and destruction of civil aircraft run into millions of dollars every year.

The cost of deterrence is also mounting. Screening against bombs at airports in the United States alone cost the airport authorities in the late 1970s nearly $200 million over a period of three years. Although these costs are high, they are not excessive. It costs the state less every year to deal with the victims of terrorism than it does in compensation for industrial accidents or the prevention of deaths on the road. Terrorism is still newsworthy because it is not an everyday occurrence.

A war of nerves?

Its psychological costs are more difficult to assess. The intensity of terrorist campaigns varies considerably: from that in Northern Ireland which has been going on since 1969, to the "sniping" war undertaken by groups of both the far left and far right in Italy which occasionally involves larger numbers, as in the bombing of the Bologna train station in 1980.

A war of nerves, of course, can be as costly as a campaign designed to inflict material losses. Terrorist activity can substantially lower the quality of life in a community, alter the attitudes or minds of those exposed to its dangers and make normal life all but impossible. This has certainly happened in Lebanon; it also appears to have occurred, to a less dramatic extent, in the two regions of Europe which have been most exposed to a sustained terrorist campaign: Northern Ireland and the Basque region of Spain.

More extreme forms

Despite all the costs, terrorism still affects relatively few people, far fewer than the 20,000 people murdered every year in the United States, a country which has learned to live with a level of violence which would have been regarded as unacceptable 50 years ago. However, there are signs that terrorism is on the increase and that people are losing confidence in their own government's ability to deal with it. At present, there are over 40 counter-terrorist companies in the United States and many others around the world, offering a variety of special services.

Another disturbing development could be that the more extreme terrorists might turn to new technologies involving the use of chemical, biological or even nuclear weapons. Several incidents have already occurred, although none with significant consequences. In 1970 a group of radicals attempted to blackmail an officer in the US Army's biological warfare center to steal some biological weapons. Two college students plotted to introduce typhoid fever into the Chicago water supply in 1972.

Since 1976, there have been a number of incidents in the United States in which small quantities of radioactive material have been lost or stolen from hospitals or research institutes. None of these thefts has been of weapons material or other equipment which would present a significant danger to large sections of the population. But in Italy the police only just foiled a plot by neo-Fascist (right-wing) extremists to introduce radioactive material into the water supply of a number of selected cities in 1974.

Nuclear terrorism

The manufacture of a nuclear bomb is another matter entirely. But it would not be beyond a group of 10 or 20 people, each skilled in such fields as nuclear physics, chemical engineering and explosives, to produce such a bomb. The cost of a laboratory, plutonium and associated equipment would vary from $50,000 to $100,000. The theft of an actual weapon or weapons grade material, while more difficult to organize, would of course, require less effort and technical skill.

The dangers of such an outcome should not be exaggerated, nor should they be underestimated. States can, at least, control the use of force; terrorist movements often cannot. Most states using nuclear weapons would be vulnerable to a counterattack and would also be answerable for the consequences of their own actions; terrorists usually are not, as the police seldom identify or locate them. This fundamental imbalance in the use of force between state and non-state means that it is impossible for the state to restrain a determined terrorist. Ultimately, a terrorist group intent on using nuclear weapons may not necessarily be deterred.

Innocent victims

To this extent, modern terrorists differ from the bomb-throwing anarchists of old in wielding power far in excess of anything their predecessors could have imagined. A hundred years ago, the victims of terrorism would have been counted, at most, in hundreds; now their numbers could be hundreds of thousands. New technologies could also place within the terrorists' reach weapons of mass destruction, the ability to create even greater uncontrollable and irreversible events.

Even so, there is cause for optimism. So far, few terrorists have displayed such suicidal tendencies. The modern political terrorist does not feel that he or she is fighting a totally hopeless cause; by and large, their aim is to win political legitimacy through the selective use of violence, aimed at particular targets or social groups. By mounting attacks using the ultimate weapon, they would completely forfeit public support. The death of too many innocents would end in complete alienation rather than intimidation, a constraint that could prevent an uncontrollable spread of the terrorist threat.

Containing the threat

But this is not the only constraint, for since the emergence of "international terrorism" in the early 1970s, characterized by the links between various groups and the spread of targets worldwide, the countries under threat have not been idle. In response to the danger, such countries have adopted policies designed to protect vulnerable targets or, in situations of extreme threat, to counterattack the terrorists or their base. Although the results have not been universally successful, enough has been achieved to make the task of the terrorist more difficult and much more dangerous.

In a society which allows freedom of movement, expression, association and political belief, the terrorist can travel, put forward views, form alliances and set up political "front" organizations with relative ease. As the IRA has shown, its ideas can be spread through newspapers and television programs in Britain, while its fund-raising efforts in the United States can be coordinated through the "charity" NORAID.

NORAID supporters in New York, 1982. Bobby Sands died while on an IRA hunger strike in jail in Northern Ireland.

A free society?

Presented with such a situation, the liberal democracy faces a dilemma, for if it takes the obvious steps to curtail these freedoms, it could end up becoming repressive and forfeiting the right to be called either liberal or truly democratic. Indeed, this may well be part of the aim of the terrorists, forcing a democratic society to change by driving a wedge between the government and the ordinary people.

If freedom of movement were to be controlled, for example, it would inevitably affect everyone in the society, not just the very small number of dissidents it was aiming to isolate and destroy. As ordinary people were forced to accept a greater degree of government control through identity checks or vehicle searches, they might well feel alienated and refuse to give their support to the anti-terrorist campaign.

Eventually, a "climate of collapse" would emerge, out of which the terrorists could gain their political demands. To a certain extent, this seemed to happen in West Germany in the early 1970s, as the government responded to the threat posed by perhaps no more than a dozen active Baader-Meinhof terrorists; it certainly happened in Uruguay in 1971, where government actions against the Tupamaros led to public alienation that was only curtailed by a military takeover of the state and the introduction of an extremely repressive system under which public opinion no longer mattered.

Government responses

The government has therefore to be extremely careful in its reaction to terrorism, although this does not mean that it can do nothing. As long as its actions have the backing of the majority of the people, as expressed

Members of the German GSG9 practice storming a building during an exercise in 1984.

through their representatives in Parliament, laws can be passed to cope with the problem. In Britain, for example, the public revulsion at the Birmingham pub bombs in November 1974, planted by the IRA, allowed the government of the day to rush through Parliament the Prevention of Terrorism Act. This act gave police wider powers to deal with terrorists and all but suspended *Habeas Corpus* (the right of individuals to be released from police custody in 24 hours unless charged with a specific crime). Similarly, in West Germany, the people were persuaded that stringent restrictions were essential if society was to survive the threat from the Baader-Meinhof Gang.

In such an atmosphere of public support, governments can go further, using selective violence in direct response to terrorist acts. Most Western states now have specialized military or paramilitary units, trained specifically for counter-terrorist operations, which they are prepared to use to rescue hostages even outside their national boundaries.

The Israelis began the process in early July 1976, when elements of their parachute forces flew all the way to Entebbe in Uganda to rescue Jewish hostages seized in a plane hijacking by members of the Popular Front for the Liberation of Palestine (PFLP) and Baader-Meinhof Gang. Landing by surprise in long-range C-130 Hercules transport aircraft, the paratroopers not only freed the hostages but also killed the terrorists guarding them and fought a gun battle with Ugandan soldiers protecting the airfield. It was a dramatic and successful operation.

The Mogadishu operation and Iranian siege

A similar mission was carried out by members of West Germany's *Grenzschutzgruppe Neun* (GSG9) at Mogadishu in Somalia in October 1977, during which 87 passengers and crew were rescued and three terrorists killed. In this particular case, the commandos were helped by men from Britain's 22nd Special Air Service Regiment (22 SAS), and it was they who, three years later, carried out the most public anti-terrorist operation to date.

On May 5, 1980, in the full glare of television cameras, SAS men in black helmets stormed the Iranian embassy in Princes Gate, London, to free hostages being held by Arab extremists intent on gaining political recognition for the Iranian province of Khuzestan. In the aftermath of this operation, it began to seem as if ruthless yet selective counter-violence was the answer to the terrorist threat.

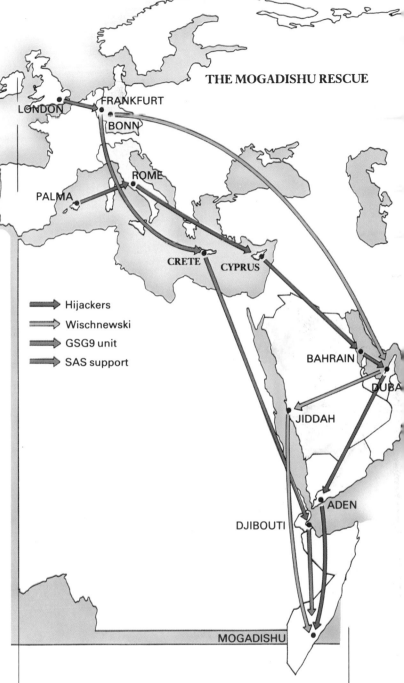

THE MOGADISHU RESCUE

Hijackers
Wischnewski
GSG9 unit
SAS support

FRANKFURT
LONDON
BONN
ROME
PALMA
CRETE
CYPRUS
BAHRAIN
DUBAI
JIDDAH
ADEN
DJIBOUTI
MOGADISHU

On October 13, 1977 Lufthansa Flight 181, a Boeing 737 flying from Majorca to Frankfurt, was hijacked and diverted to Rome. The four terrorists demanded the release of Baader-Meinhof Gang leaders, held in West Germany, then flew to Bahrain and Dubai, followed by a West German negotiator, Hans-Jurgen Wischnewski, and GSG9 commandos. At Aden on October 16, the 737 pilot was killed and the aircraft routed to Mogadishu. It was here that the GSG9 assault, aided by two SAS men from London, took place early on October 18. All the hostages were freed.

Failures

But this was a false presumption. As early as March 1978, elements of Egypt's Sa'Aqa ("Lightning") commando group had failed to rescue hostages being held on board a hijacked aircraft on the airfield at Larnaca in Cyprus (they had failed to coordinate their actions with the local authorities and were, quite understandably, fired upon by the Cypriot National Guard as they approached the plane). Indeed, the record of Sa'Aqa is a salutary one, for their attempt to storm another hijacked aircraft, this time at Luqa in Malta, in December 1985, left 59 of the hostages dead as the terrorists opened fire.

Nor should it be presumed that the Western democracies are universally successful: in April 1980, only weeks before the SAS operation at Princes Gate, the American rescue mission to Tehran (Operation Eagle Claw) ended in disaster in the Iranian desert as helicopters proved unable to cope with the extremes of climate and terrain involved.

Anti-terrorist measures

The precarious nature of such a use of counter-force, coupled to the obvious effects that failure will have on the credibility of the government in the eyes of the people, means that countries must look for other approaches if they are to minimize the impact of terrorism. One possibility is to protect the targets of terrorism more carefully, denying the terrorists the chance of planting bombs or seizing hostages. Searches of passengers at airport departure lounges, the deployment of armed soldiers or policemen around airfields and the policy of arming special guards to travel "shot-gun" on board aircraft in flight have all been tried and have enjoyed some success, but they will have only limited effect if restricted to individual countries or airlines.

Sharing information is an important aspect of international cooperation in the fight against terrorism. The United States, Great Britain and Germany have set up computer banks to store information about terrorist groups. This has been greatly helped by advances in new technology.

Of much more effect would be close cooperation between countries, based upon a universal condemnation of terrorism as a political instrument. However, too many countries either sympathize with the aims of groups such as the PLO or are afraid to offer condemnation in case it should leave them vulnerable to attack.

Helicopter wreckage in the Iranian desert, after the failure of the American rescue mission.

X-ray machines in airports detect guns.

International cooperation

But it would be wrong to presume that no attempts have been made to gain international agreements. At various times since the early 1970s, the United Nations has tried to adopt resolutions condemning terrorism (only to fail in the face of opposition from countries, particularly in the Middle East, which support the Palestinian cause). The EEC, however, has accepted a Six-Point Counter-Terrorism Agreement (1976) which is meant to coordinate the actions of member states, following it up with a Convention on Terrorism (1977) designed to increase the impact.

The record of success is small, with no guarantees that signatory states will abide by the conditions imposed, and in the end, it has been left to individual countries to sort out their own problems. Some have done so very effectively, seeking out like-minded states to negotiate bilateral counter-terrorist moves. Thus, for example, Britain has persuaded President Ronald Reagan to curtail the activities of NORAID, widely felt to be raising money for the purchase of arms for the IRA in Northern Ireland. This action was reinforced by a new Extradition Treaty which permits the return of those who face a charge of terrorist action to the country where it took place.

A similar treaty has also been negotiated between Britain and Eire (Southern Ireland), so that terrorist suspects can no longer gain asylum by claiming that their actions were politically motivated. France has always followed this line, refusing to extradite known terrorists if they claimed political asylum. This may change in view of the bomb attacks on Paris in September 1986 and the conviction of the Lebanese terrorist Georges Abdallah for terrorist crimes in February 1987.

The future

The response to terrorism sets an exceptionally difficult problem, especially in the Western democracies. Ideally, the threat of international attack should elicit an international response, but this has proved virtually impossible to effect, forcing threatened states to find their own means of protection. Some have successfully deployed special forces to take the "war" to the terrorists, rescuing hostages and attacking bases in foreign countries, but this can go wrong. An alternative is the negotiation of bilateral agreements to counter the worst of the problem, and here the record is comparatively good. If this can be used as a basis for more general agreements, leading eventually to international responses, terrorism may yet be defeated.

Thus, for example, when Britain sought support for her decision to cut off diplomatic relations with Syria in October 1986, after the latter country was implicated in a plot to blow up an Israeli aircraft at Heathrow, the response from the Western Europeans was by no means unanimous. Greece, long sympathetic to the Arab cause, refused to do anything, and France, in the throes of a particularly lucrative arms deal with Iran, using Syria as "middle-man," showed a distinct lack of enthusiasm for policies any stronger than EEC trade sanctions.

As might be expected, the aims of individual countries tend to take precedence over the interests of the international community. The Americans discovered this in April 1986 when they received little support for their air attacks on Libya. These were designed to destroy terrorist bases in the aftermath of a spate of anti-American actions by groups supposed to be backed by Colonel Gaddafi.

A Security Council session.

CHAPTER 4
REGULATING CONFLICT

Solutions to international problems are hard to find, but the United Nations offers a forum for debate and a center for negotiation rather than force. Unfortunately, it tends to reflect the power and influence of the established Northern countries and its record of success in solving world problems is poor. The best that may be achieved is "peace-keeping" rather than "peace-making," with United Nations' forces imposing and monitoring ceasefires instead of preventing violence.

"That we have this Charter is a great wonder," President Harry Truman of the United States told the First Session of the United Nations (UN) when it met in San Francisco in 1945. It is perhaps an even greater wonder that the United Nations has survived for over 40 years, and that it has developed to a point where it represents the interests of 159 (out of 167) states in the modern world.

The UN Charter

The United Nations was created to act as the highest international authority for resolving disputes and maintaining the peace. Signed by a total of 51 countries on June 26, 1945, its Charter requires its members to settle conflicts by peaceful means, and to refer them to a Security Council of major powers if they cannot reach agreement. On occasions, the Council has acted on its own account, dispatching peacekeeping forces or applying sanctions (the cutting of trade links to isolate a country economically is one of these) against regimes in breach of the rules. It has proved less successful in punishing governments for abusing human rights or dealing with terrorist groups who have often drawn upon the support of its own members.

The Charter had to be highly flexible in order to reconcile the different ideological beliefs of the two superpowers, the United States and the Soviet Union, who soon found themselves at odds after the defeat of Germany and Japan in 1945. Anxious to provide the new organization with some authority, the original members of the United Nations gave the Security Council some powers but required the unanimous consent of the five permanent members (the victors in 1945: the United States, the Soviet Union, Great Britain, France and China). The Security Council is supposed to deal with threats to peace and has some power to enforce its decisions.

Since 1945, the Security Council has been increased to 15 members – the additional 10 are chosen from the rest of the members of the United Nations on a rotational basis. They serve for a period of two years but do not enjoy the right of veto (refusal to accept suggested resolutions). The members left for future discussion the task of raising a military force. This was indefinitely deferred after the United States and the Soviet Union failed to reach agreement at the London Conference of 1946.

The General Assembly

To obtain the consent of the majority of members who had seats in the General Assembly (the main body of the United Nations, in which all members have an equal voice) the Council allowed the Assembly a broad power of discussion. But its authority was limited from the beginning to recommendations only, it being argued that this would prevent the adoption of ideological or regional preferences and so encourage the development of unbiased views, essential to the task of maintaining and promoting the peace.

Other articles in the UN Charter committed members to settle their disputes peacefully and not through the threatened use of force. To diminish the underlying causes of conflict, the Charter also provided for economic and social progress, the promotion of human rights and other matters. Subsidiary organizations, such as the United Nations Educational Scientific and Cultural Organization (UNESCO), the World Health Organization (WHO) and the International Monetary Fund (IMF) have been set up to advance these aims and aspirations. Their success has depended on the support they get from their members.

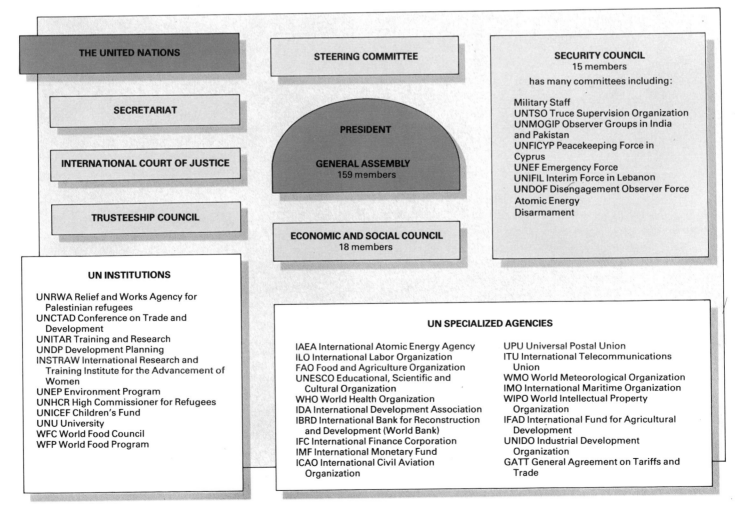

THE UNITED NATIONS

SECRETARIAT

INTERNATIONAL COURT OF JUSTICE

TRUSTEESHIP COUNCIL

STEERING COMMITTEE

PRESIDENT

GENERAL ASSEMBLY
159 members

ECONOMIC AND SOCIAL COUNCIL
18 members

SECURITY COUNCIL
15 members
has many committees including:

Military Staff
UNTSO Truce Supervision Organization
UNMOGIP Observer Groups in India and Pakistan
UNFICYP Peacekeeping Force in Cyprus
UNEF Emergency Force
UNIFIL Interim Force in Lebanon
UNDOF Disengagement Observer Force
Atomic Energy
Disarmament

UN INSTITUTIONS

UNRWA Relief and Works Agency for Palestinian refugees
UNCTAD Conference on Trade and Development
UNITAR Training and Research
UNDP Development Planning
INSTRAW International Research and Training Institute for the Advancement of Women
UNEP Environment Program
UNHCR High Commissioner for Refugees
UNICEF Children's Fund
UNU University
WFC World Food Council
WFP World Food Program

UN SPECIALIZED AGENCIES

IAEA International Atomic Energy Agency
ILO International Labor Organization
FAO Food and Agriculture Organization
UNESCO Educational, Scientific and Cultural Organization
WHO World Health Organization
IDA International Development Association
IBRD International Bank for Reconstruction and Development (World Bank)
IFC International Finance Corporation
IMF International Monetary Fund
ICAO International Civil Aviation Organization

UPU Universal Postal Union
ITU International Telecommunications Union
WMO World Meteorological Organization
IMO International Maritime Organization
WIPO World Intellectual Property Organization
IFAD International Fund for Agricultural Development
UNIDO Industrial Development Organization
GATT General Agreement on Tariffs and Trade

Why has the United Nations survived?

From the start the United Nations has been criticized as an institution that has failed to live up to the aspirations and hopes of the founding members. It is possible to argue that it has not achieved much, that the superpowers have used the United Nations as an arena in which to compete rather than resolve their differences. This contradicts one of the United Nations' main functions as "a center for harmonizing the actions of nations" (Article 1(4) UN Charter).

But unlike its predecessor, the League of Nations (founded in 1920), it has not been ignored; and that perhaps is the most important contribution that it has made to the resolution of conflict. It is precisely because the United Nations is of value to the superpowers and their allies that it has been used by them.

The key to the United Nations' survival has been the extent to which the permanent members of the Security Council have acted to gain and retain control. In the first 30 years of its existence, the General Assembly passed 3,500 resolutions, the great majority of which were totally ignored by the Council. Despite a shift in voting patterns with the emergence of a new Afro-Asian majority in the General Assembly after 1960, the victors of 1945 are still in control. Indeed, it is as well to remember that Italy only became a member in 1955, Japan in 1956 and the two Germanies as late as the year 1973.

The Security Council

The power of the Security Council lies in several fields. Only the Council has a veto on resolutions. The Secretary-General can only be appointed with the approval of all its members, an important condition that denied the post to Max Jakobson in 1971 because of opposition from the Soviet Union, and to the Tanzanian Foreign Minister Salim Salim in 1982 because of opposition from the United States.

The Council is the only body that can deny membership to any state or make a new state a member. Until 1971 the United States successfully kept out communist China, while China in turn successfully blocked Bangladesh's membership for three years. The veto of the three Western powers (the United States, Great Britain and France) has kept South Africa a member since the motion to expel it was first adopted by the General Assembly in 1974.

In the process of control, the use of abstentions has played a major role. By abstaining (refusing to vote) rather than vetoing (voting against) a motion, the five permanent members have been able to support each other without the embarrassment of being too closely associated with one another's actions.

It was the Soviets who, at the first Security Council in London in 1946, insisted that abstention should not necessarily constitute a veto. Over the years the Chinese have abstained on placing UN forces in the Sinai but have not used the veto. Similarly, the Soviet Union has regularly abstained whenever the maintenance of United Nations forces in Cyprus has been debated, without wishing to vote against a peacekeeping presence.

The Third World

That is not to say that the General Assembly lacks punch. It can embarrass members of the Security Council, as it did with the Soviet Union in the Hungarian crisis of 1956 and over the invasion of Afghanistan in 1979. More often the West has found itself out on a limb on such matters as South Africa's membership, with no less than 91 members voting for expulsion in 1974. Finally, the Afro-Asian bloc, acting in unison, has been able to place on the Security Council's agenda issues which the West in particular would prefer to have ignored.

Since 1960, apartheid in South Africa has been regularly debated. Since 1968, the United Nations has been intimately involved in the negotiations to transfer power in Namibia (Southwest Africa) from South Africa to representatives of the local people. Resolutions may not be accepted by the Council unless put forward as a Resolution for Peace after the Council has failed to act in a particular crisis, but their passage and continual emphasis has produced a form of international public policy.

The General Assembly's resolutions may not constitute international law, but they are now recognized by the International Court of Justice in The Hague as customary law, and therefore worth taking into consideration by other countries. That in itself constitutes one of the United Nations' greatest advances.

Of equal importance has been the absorption of over 100 "new" states since 1945. For as they have emerged, their membership of the General Assembly has not only given them a place in the world order but also a voice in world affairs. The role of the United Nations as a political "forum" for debate, in which grievances can at least be heard and diplomatic contacts established, should not be ignored.

The Palestinian problem

Nevertheless, it is in the role of peace-keeping that the United Nations catches the public eye, and here the successes of the organization are mixed, as may be seen most forcibly in the Middle East. The problem began with the independence of Palestine and the United States' refusal to accept the General Assembly's 1947 plan for the country's partition into separate Jewish and Arab states. The United States objected to the possible role of a peacekeeping force which might include Soviet soldiers and was conscious of domestic pressure from a strong Jewish political "lobby." The Palestine problem was not the first time the two superpowers clashed in the United Nations, but it was by far the most important.

The Palestine debacle highlighted two lessons which have remained central ever since. First, the United Nations can only prevent the outbreak of war if the Security Council is prepared to act. Second, the failure to agree on the causes of conflict because of deep-seated ideological differences between the Council's Western members and the Soviet Union makes it inevitable that, even if the United Nations succeeds in keeping the peace, it can not possibly hope to create it. At best violence might be contained, but conflict as such can only be postponed, not preempted.

Indeed, this is precisely what happened in Palestine. Unable to agree on a peace plan, the United Nations found itself unable either to prevent the state of Israel from coming into being on May 15, 1948 or from being attacked on the same day by its Arab neighbors. Once war had broken out, it was reduced to imposing a ceasefire agreement, monitoring demilitarized zones and supervising the eventual truce. The problem itself persisted.

The Arab-Israeli Wars

When war between Israel and Egypt flared up again in 1956, the United Nations set out to divide the two forces by maintaining a semipermanent mission in the two principal areas of tension: the Gaza Strip and the Sinai desert. Eleven years later, when the Egyptians decided to test the issue again by massing forces in Sinai, they asked the United Nations' monitoring team to withdraw from the area, a request with which the United Nations had no option but to comply: after all, like all UN forces, it could only be deployed at the "invitation" of the host country, in this case Egypt. Concluding that the Egyptians had resolved to press home their advantage, the Israeli government chose attack as the best means of defense. The result was the Six-Day War of 1967.

An Israeli column passes Egyptian troops, captured in the Sinai desert, 1967.

The result of a devastating truck-bomb attack on the command post of US and French peacekeeping forces, Lebanon, 1983.

The United Nations has been involved in the Middle East since 1947 and has deployed peacekeeping or observer forces since 1956. In the aftermath of the 1973 "Yom Kippur" War, UN observers were sent to monitor ceasefire lines in Sinai and on the Golan Heights; five years later a special UNIFIL force was committed to southern Lebanon after clashes between Israeli troops and the PLO. The Sinai observers were withdrawn in 1979 but the others remain.

UN PEACEKEEPING FORCES IN THE MIDDLE EAST

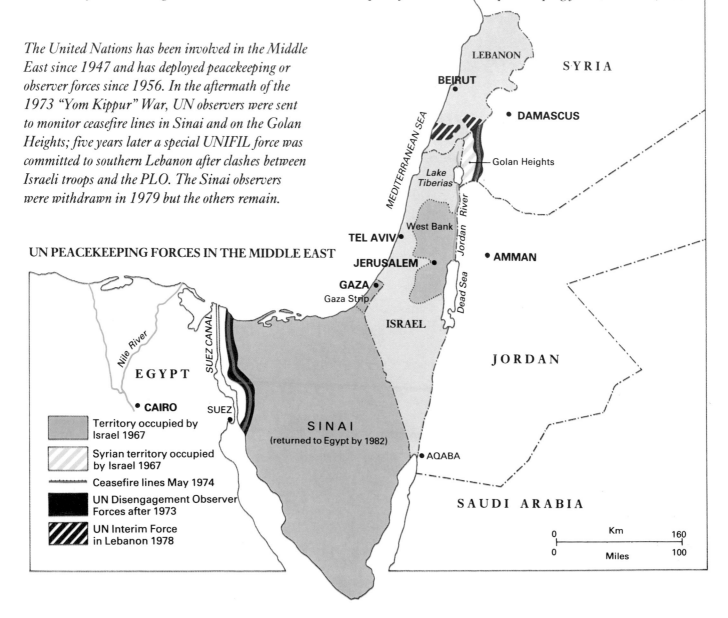

Legend:
- Territory occupied by Israel 1967
- Syrian territory occupied by Israel 1967
- Ceasefire lines May 1974
- UN Disengagement Observer Forces after 1973
- UN Interim Force in Lebanon 1978

Map labels: LEBANON, SYRIA, BEIRUT, DAMASCUS, MEDITERRANEAN SEA, Golan Heights, Lake Tiberias, Jordan River, West Bank, TEL AVIV, AMMAN, JERUSALEM, GAZA, Gaza Strip, Dead Sea, ISRAEL, JORDAN, Nile River, SUEZ CANAL, EGYPT, CAIRO, SUEZ, SINAI (returned to Egypt by 1982), AQABA, SAUDI ARABIA

Scale: 0 — Km — 160; 0 — Miles — 100

Throughout that conflict, the United Nations was powerless to intervene. Indeed, it only succeeded in arranging a ceasefire after the Israelis had achieved their immediate objectives: the capture of the Sinai peninsula, the West Bank of the Jordan River and the Golan Heights of Syria. It took a further five months before it could even agree to draft Resolution 242 (November 22, 1967) which called upon both parties to sign a comprehensive peace treaty. Even then, no one could agree whether the resolution required Israel to withdraw in advance of the negotiations, to withdraw from some or all of the occupied territories simultaneously or to seek a negotiated withdrawal to "secure and recognized boundaries free from threats or acts of force." A special UN representative was sent to talk to the countries concerned, to help reach a settlement.

The 1973 War

The situation was still left unresolved when the next major Arab-Israeli war broke out on October 6, 1973. Again the Security Council failed to prevent the outbreak of the conflict, although it was clear that both Egypt and Syria would eventually try to regain the land they had lost. The Soviet Union was even unwilling to consider a ceasefire until it had become clear that, after their initial success, the Arab armies were about to suffer a serious defeat. Thus, although the Council first met to discuss the issue on October 8 at the request of the United States, it was not until October 22 that it agreed to take action, passing Resolution 338 which required both parties to stop fighting and sign a treaty. Even then, the Israelis chose to ignore the ceasefire for a further 48 hours, during which time they consolidated their positions on the west bank of the Suez Canal.

The 1973 War illustrated two themes very clearly: that the Security Council could act decisively to end a war, but equally that it could not create a lasting peace. In an attempt to prevent the outbreak of yet another war, the United States tried to make peace between Israel and Egypt permanent by embarking on a series of negotiations which were to lead first to the disengagement of rival forces (1974-75) and then to a separate peace treaty between the two powers (1979). Although the UN Disengagement Observer Force (UNDOF) played a role in supervising the ceasefire in May 1974, the United States was left to press ahead with its more ambitious schemes alone.

In the words of a US official in 1975, the United States' aim was "not just to disentangle their (Arab and

Israeli) forces in the aftermath of war but to commit them to the peaceful resolution of the differences that have so long made them mortal enemies." The United Nations has been unable to make this happen.

The Korean War

Only once has the United Nations attempted to make peace, rather than keep it, and that was in June 1950 at the time of the Korean War. In response to the communist invasion of the South, the United Nations followed up its order to the North Koreans to withdraw with a decision to dispatch a UN force led and funded by the United States. The Soviets were not present when the vote was taken as they had walked out in protest against the American refusal to recognize the People's Republic of China. Fifteen governments eventually contributed to the force; many others made contributions of non-military equipment.

When UN forces reached the frontier between the two countries, the 38th parallel, the United States and the UN Secretary-General took the view that unless UN forces crossed into the North, the fighting might break out at any time; that it might be better to deal with the problem once and for all by overthrowing the government of Kim Il Sung rather than acquiesce in the permanent division of Korea.

To this end the Americans introduced a resolution which was subsequently adopted by the General Assembly, recommending that all necessary steps should be taken to ensure that peace was enforced throughout Korea, a measure that enabled them to prosecute the war more vigorously. In the event, of course, the decision to cross the 38th parallel merely precipitated Chinese intervention and prolonged the conflict for another three years.

Never again was the United Nations to pay the price of making the peace, in part because it had proved so dauntingly high. In the three months during which the United Nations found itself in occupation of the larger part of North Korea, 100,000 citizens were "executed" or killed. More bombs were dropped on the North than had been dropped on Germany in five years of war. UN prisoner-of-war camps were so badly run that the inmates and guards often found themselves engaged in pitched battles. The cost of making the peace seemed higher than the cost of keeping it. The United Nations was seen as backing a brutal and relentless conflict on the part of a government that in retrospect seemed almost as bad, in the opinion of many, as the government of the aggressor.

The Falklands War

Yet it would be wrong to assume that the record has been entirely negative. The support the United Kingdom received in the run-up to the Falklands War in 1982 did much to restore the United Nations' reputation in parts of the Western world.

Somewhat to its own surprise, perhaps, Britain received almost unanimous international support when Argentina occupied the Falklands in April 1982 after years of negotiations between the two powers had failed. The Security Council roundly condemned the occupation and rejected Argentina's claim that the requirement under the UN Charter to settle disputes peacefully did not apply to quarrels that predated the Charter's adoption. As the British representative noted, had this been accepted, the world would have become a more dangerous place.

The Council went on to reject a further Argentinian claim that it was entitled to resort to force because of the strength of its legal claim to sovereignty of the islands, a claim that had been endorsed on many occasions by the UN Committee on Decolonization. Instead, the Council insisted that the only justification for force could be self-defense.

Although it did not condemn the invasion as an act of aggression, by demanding Argentina's immediate withdrawal (Resolution 502) it was making it clear that Argentina's actions were illegal. Some weeks later a British Task Force retook the islands. Even if the United Nations did not resolve the conflict, it created circumstances in which Britain's use of force could be seen in terms of the defense of international law.

Peacekeeping forces

The sending in of peacekeeping forces has been used not so much to resolve conflicts as to reduce tensions between states (for example, India and Pakistan in Kashmir in 1965) or even communities (for example, Greek and Turkish Cypriots in 1964). The exercise may have value, but the number of occasions on which the peacekeeping forces have been used have been few and far between.

Even when they are committed, the practical problems of gathering forces acceptable to all parties in a particular dispute are often immense. So too are the problems of financing, commanding and coordinating the different contingents and of deciding what role they are to play.

UN Peacekeeping Force in Cyprus, 1974. Since 1964 it has tried to prevent fighting between the Greeks and Turks.

Captured Argentine soldiers, Falkland Islands, 1982.

Sanctions

Whenever the UN wishes to act decisively against a state in breach of international law or which has defied the terms of the UN Charter, it does have a more immediate weapon on hand: that of economic sanctions, although they have been used only sparingly. When they were incorporated in the Charter they were intended to do no more than make life difficult for a country's citizens, and to undermine political morale and the legitimacy of a particular regime. They were not intended to be a form of economic warfare. Their aim was more modest if no less difficult: to persuade a government to change its policies, not necessarily to overthrow it completely.

Trade sanctions have been used once by the United Nations: against the government of Rhodesia after its Unilateral Declaration of Independence (UDI) from Britain in 1965. They failed for several reasons, principally because, far from undermining popular support for Prime Minister Ian Smith, they increased it. The feeling of being under siege often helps sustain a government's will to resist. It can also be a useful excuse for a regime to introduce such unpopular measures as rationing people's spending ability and increasing taxation. This is precisely what happened in the case of Rhodesia.

Second, sanctions are usually only effective if they are accompanied by a variety of other measures: military pressure, isolating the country from contacts with the outside world, or stronger economic instruments. Otherwise they may only serve to encourage greater inventiveness and productivity on the part of a beleaguered state.

During the Second World War, for example, the German economy responded to a much sharper economic siege with remarkable success by pioneering some of the most significant breakthroughs in synthetic fuels and the use of ferro-alloys in reinforcing steel. Some 25 years later, from a much weaker technical and industrial base, Rhodesia witnessed a dramatic expansion in the production of ferro-chrome for refined steel products. Sanctions failed, in short, because they had the unintended effect of making the country more self-sufficient, not less.

Third, the international community tends to wait far too long before introducing comprehensive sanctions, usually until it has been frustrated in its earlier efforts. Even in Rhodesia, when stiffer economic penalties were introduced they only began to have a marked impact on productivity when they were combined with a sustained guerrilla war after 1972. It was this combined pressure which finally forced the government to the conference table in 1979.

Finally, no government can afford to lose sight of its own national interests in defense of international law. In the case of Rhodesia, the United States felt that it was in no position to deny itself imports of non-fuel minerals such as chrome, or 72 other metals which were specifically exempt from the embargo by act of Congress in 1972.

Terrorism and human rights

Apart from the case of Rhodesia, the United Nations has singularly failed to deal directly with actions that have outraged the "conscience of mankind." It has done very little, for example, to curb international terrorism either on the part of terrorist groups or, more worrying still, on the part of those governments which have occasionally supported them.

The international community, of course, had tried to draw up codes of conduct laying down rules against terrorism long before the United Nations came into being. The first international convention against terrorism in 1937, which was signed by 23 countries, sought the compulsory extradition or prosecution of all fugitives accused of "political terrorism," especially assassination. Yet terrorism was defined so broadly that the convention was never ratified (accepted) and, therefore, never came into force.

The Draft Code of Offenses against the Peace and Security of Mankind which was first drawn up by the International Law Commission in 1954 has still not been ratified. Originally the General Assembly found itself so divided that it deferred consideration of the report indefinitely. It has never resumed any of these discussions.

The Entebbe raid

In the case where individual governments are accused of terrorism, this omission has been especially regrettable. Where the signatories to the UN Charter have themselves broken the rules, the United Nations' failure to act has been inexcusable. Its reaction to recent events may offer slight grounds for hope, but it is constantly undermined by a general lack of agreement as to what is the best way of proceeding to deal with any problems.

Some of the passengers, rescued during the Entebbe raid, arrive home, 1976.

In June 1976, for example, the United Nations chose not to act at all when PFLP and Baader-Meinhof terrorists hijacked an Air France plane to Entebbe with 250 passengers, including 96 Israelis, on board. Its reaction to the subsequent Israeli rescue mission in early July was equally worrying. The raid was immediately condemned by the African states at the United Nations as a flagrant attack on Ugandan sovereignty, a clear "act of aggression." For their part, the Israelis insisted that they had the right of self-defense, the right to protect their own nationals in a situation in which the government of another country was clearly unwilling to do so. They further argued that Uganda had violated the 1970 Hague Convention which required its signatories to prosecute or extradite all hijackers.

The ensuing debate in the Security Council proved inconclusive, and Israel won no more than a moral victory (it was not censured and the debate brought out the full extent of Uganda's complicity with the hijackers). When it came to the vote, the sponsors of the motion condemning Israel preferred to abstain rather than defend Uganda's actions, but the United Nations failed to condemn terrorism.

The Iranian hostage crisis

The second occasion in which the United Nations became involved was the Iranian hostage crisis in 1979. This occurred when Muslim fundamentalists overthrew the Shah of Iran, who was given asylum in the United States. In protest, 52 Americans were seized and held hostage by Iranian students on November 4, 1979. The Iranian government did nothing to prevent this action, which violated the rules of normal diplomatic relations between countries.

The United Nations, to its credit, upheld the American case from the very beginning. On November 9 it called unanimously for the unconditional release of all the hostages. In an interim order on December 15 the International Court of Justice (ICJ) ordered their immediate release, upholding that judgment in its final verdict on May 24, 1980.

In international law, however, the Security Council is not bound to carry out the rulings of the ICJ. Even if this had not been the case, the Soviet veto would have prevented the United Nations from imposing sanctions. As a result it could be claimed that once again the United Nations not only failed its own members but also betrayed the high hopes of those who set it up. Once again, by its inaction it forced the victim (the

United States) to resort to force, although on this occasion the US rescue mission in April 1980 was disastrously unsuccessful. In the end, the United States had to accept apparently humiliating terms to gain the release of its nationals in January 1981.

But at least when the crisis was at its height, the General Assembly unanimously adopted an International Convention against the taking of hostages. This was an important step because it contained new elements which were not to be found in any other anti-terrorist conventions. These included the clear rejection of the idea that small states were entitled to break international law.

The hostage crisis may not have won the United States the support it had hoped for. However it did demonstrate that there was a point beyond which a Third World state could not expect support even from its fellow members. Clearly the phrase "global village" counted for something when some countries chose to act against the "general interest" of all.

Unfortunately, there has been little evidence since then to suggest that the countries prepared to support the convention are willing or able to act. Terrorist groups still find sponsors among countries which are members of the General Assembly and concerted, international responses to terrorism have still to emerge. It is not an impressive record.

Conclusion

In the light of the high expectations entertained by the founding fathers when they met to draw up the Charter at San Francisco in 1945, the United Nations may, therefore, be said to have failed. But the world in which it has operated was not one they could ever have imagined. Given the grave ideological differences between the superpowers and the pace of political and economic change in the past 30 years, the organization has not done too badly. Its failures have not been necessarily of its own making; its success has been to have survived and to have been used by the superpowers, rather than ignored by them.

This is not an unimportant achievement, given the fact that the fate of its predecessor, the League of Nations, was that its more powerful members declined to use it at all. As long as the United Nations exists and is taken seriously, even as nothing more than a forum for debate, the world is a safer place, but the problems facing it, particularly in terms of resource rivalry, the North-South divide and terrorism, are immense. We still have a long way to go before creating a safer world.

CONFLICT IN THE 20TH CENTURY: APPENDICES

Modern conflict often ignores national boundaries, affecting the world as a whole rather than individual countries. Competition for natural resources produces tensions which constantly threaten war, while the actions of terrorist groups and of special forces raised to counter them creates a backcloth of violence. In such circumstances, as the United Nations searches desperately for solutions, the role of personalities can be crucial.

PERSONALITIES

Yasser Arafat (1929-). Chairman of the Palestine Liberation Organization and leader of *Fatah*. Born in British-ruled Palestine, he fled to Egypt in 1948, where he trained as an engineer. In the 1950s he moved to Kuwait, founding *Fatah* as a guerrilla group dedicated to attacks against Israeli targets. In 1969 he was elected Chairman of the PLO, a position he still holds despite the humiliation of military defeat in Lebanon (1982) and the emergence of many rivals within the Palestinian movement.

Andreas Baader (1943-77). Joint leader of the Baader-Meinhof terrorist group in West Germany. A petty criminal with a liking for fast cars, he showed little interest in politics, leaving that to student colleagues. Convicted of arson (1968), he escaped while on parole, only to be rearrested in Berlin. Rescued by Ulrike Meinhof (May 1970), Baader helped to carry out a campaign of terror which did not die down with his arrest in 1972. Sentenced to life imprisonment, he committed suicide in Stammheim Prison in October 1977.

Sabri al-Banna ("Abu Nidal") (1937-). Terrorist leader. Born in British-ruled Palestine, he fled to Gaza in 1948. He joined *Fatah* in the 1960s and, in 1970, was sent to Iraq as a PLO representative. Trained in North Korea and China, he is dedicated to the destruction of Israel. Taking the name "Abu Nidal" (Father of the Struggle), he founded a terrorist group of the same name (originally called Black June) and organized a number of operations, notably the grenade attacks on Rome and Vienna airports (December 1985).

Willy Brandt (1913-). West German politician and author of the Brandt Reports on "international development issues." An opponent of Nazism, he moved to Norway in the 1930s, returning to Germany in 1945. Elected Mayor of West Berlin (1957), he became leader of the Social Democratic Party (1960) and Chancellor of West Germany (1969). After resigning in 1974, he became deeply involved in the problems of the North-South divide. His two Reports (1980 and 1983) were important and received a lot of international coverage. However, governments did not take them up and they had little appreciable effect.

Sabri al-Banna ("Abu Nidal")

Yasser Arafat

Willy Brandt

Dag Hammarskjöld (1905-61). Secretary General of the United Nations (1953-61). Son of a prime minister of Sweden, he served in a variety of Swedish administrative posts before being chosen as UN Secretary General. His time in that office coincided with a period of doubt about the role of the United Nations, made worse by the controversial deployment of UN troops to the Congo (1961). Hammarskjöld was killed in an air crash in Northern Rhodesia (Zambia), while on a truce-making mission.

Robert McNamara (1916-). American administrator. After serving in the air force during the Second World War, he joined the Ford Motor Company, eventually becoming its president in 1960. A year later, he was appointed Secretary of Defense in President John F. Kennedy's administration. During the next seven years he was responsible for refining the US nuclear strategy of Flexible Response and for overseeing the commitment of US forces to Vietnam. After resigning in 1968, he became President of the World Bank (1969-81).

Ulrike Meinhof (1934-76). Joint leader of the Baader-Meinhof terrorist group in West Germany.

Educated at Marburg University, she became a journalist, specializing in left-wing political issues. In May 1970 she organized the rescue of Andreas Baader from prison and then went into hiding, traveling to Jordan to be trained by the PLO. After a spate of bank robberies and bomb attacks, she was arrested in June 1972 and sentenced to eight years in prison. She committed suicide in May 1976.

Ilyich Ramirez Sanchez ("Carlos") (1949-). International terrorist. Born in Venezuela, he hit the headlines in December 1975 when he led a group of Palestinian and West German terrorists in the kidnap of OPEC ministers in Vienna. Used by the Popular Front for the Liberation of Palestine as a "contact man," liaising with other terrorist groups, "Carlos" is renowned for his wealthy life-style and ruthless actions. Still at large, he was most recently held responsible for a bomb attack on Marseilles railroad station in December 1983.

U Thant (1909-74). Secretary General of the United Nations (1962-71). Born in Burma, he worked as a schoolteacher between 1928 and 1947, before becoming an adviser to the Burmese prime minister. In 1957 he became Burma's representative at the United Nations in New York and

was chosen to act as Secretary General on Hammarskjöld's death in 1961. A year later he was confirmed in the post, guiding the United Nations through the difficult period of the 1960s.

Kurt Waldheim (1918-). Secretary General of the United Nations (1972-82) and President of Austria (1986-). After service in the German Army in the Second World War, he entered the Austrian foreign service and, eventually, rose to be Minister for Foreign Affairs (1968-70). Chosen as UN Secretary General in 1972, he gained a reputation for tact and diplomatic skill. In 1986 he was elected President of Austria, despite controversy about his career.

Ulrich Wegener (1931-). Commander of West Germany's elite GSG9 anti-terrorist group during the Mogadishu rescue mission (October 1977). A member of the Federal Border Police since 1958, Wegener trained with both the FBI and the Israeli secret service before being directed to form an anti-terrorist force in 1972. By 1977, GSG9 comprised 188 highly trained specialists, well suited to hijack-rescue operations. In 1979, Wegener was promoted from colonel to brigadier and given overall command of the Border Police.

Dag Hammarskjöld

Robert McNamara

U Thant

RESOURCE RIVALRY AT SEA

Seven-tenths of the world's surface is covered by sea, and most of the important trade routes, carrying raw materials or manufactured goods from country to country, cross the major oceans. Because they are used by everyone with access to the sea (all but about 30 of the countries of the world), such routes have traditionally been regarded as "international," with no one enjoying exclusive rights. During both world wars (1914-18 and 1939-45), combatant powers such as Germany, Britain, the United States and Japan fought to exclude their enemies, using aircraft, submarines, surface fleets and mines, but in normal times merchant ships have the right to free passage.

Exploration of the seabed

More recently, two problems have emerged. First, as mineral resources such as oil or manganese begin to run out on land, countries have looked increasingly to the oceans for replacement stocks. In some cases, as in the Gulf of Mexico or the North Sea, oil exploration has taken place, with vast deposits of oil and natural gas being tapped by those countries with the money and expertise to do so; elsewhere, as in the Aegean or the waters of Antarctica, mineral deposits are known to exist, apparently waiting to be exploited.

However, if such deposits are situated in international waters, an obvious difficulty arises, for no one has the right to take them. If the minerals lie in such waters, they should belong to the world as a whole, but since only very few countries have the expertise to exploit the minerals, the only ones to profit would be those countries or their companies. This, in turn, would make the division between "rich" and "poor" worse, because only the richer countries could then afford these minerals.

Exclusive Economic Zones

One solution would be to divide the oceans into Exclusive Economic Zones (EEZs) – an idea put forward by the Law of the Sea Conference in 1982 – but this leads to the second of the major problems. EEZs might give countries complete control of mineral (and fishing) rights off their shorelines, but they could also become *total* exclusion zones in which movement was restricted or not allowed at all. Not only would this disrupt world trade, it would also lead to crises and confrontations – if not all-out wars – as countries felt that their economic livelihoods were under threat.

This would become worse if the EEZs overlapped (an inevitable consequence of 167 countries competing for access to the riches of the sea). Problems could also arise if the EEZs included so-called "choke-points" on world shipping routes.

There are many such choke-points

Resource rivalry at Sea

ARCTIC OCEAN
Barents Sea
"Cod Wars"
North Sea
Okhotsk Sea
Strait of Gibraltar
Aegean Sea
Suez Canal
Strait of Hormuz
Gulf of Mexico
ATLANTIC OCEAN
Bab el Mandeb Strait
Gulf of Oman
South China Sea
Panama Canal
Strait of Malacca
PACIFIC OCEAN
INDIAN OCEAN
Beagle Channel

Km 0   4,000
Miles 0   2,500

ANTARCTIC OCEAN

– areas of narrow ocean or man-made "canals" – and although there have been attempts in the past to make them "international," with free access to all shipping, existing agreements could be compromised if neighboring countries see the water-ways as essential economic areas.

Conflict over sea routes

Since 1948, Israel has been to war with Egypt on at least two occasions (October 1956 and June 1967) to ensure free access to the Suez Canal and to its port at Elat; Britain and Spain have failed to reach agreement over the Strait of Gibraltar; the West has moved forces to the Gulf of Oman to ensure free passage for oil tankers from the Gulf States through the Strait of Hormuz; the United States has shown grave concern about possible communist expansion in Central America towards the Panama Canal; Argentina and Chile have nearly gone to war over the Beagle Channel. Indeed, one of the reasons why the United States was so reluctant to accept the findings of the Law of the Sea Conference in 1982 was the fact that EEZs belonging to Indonesia and Malaysia threatened free passage of the Strait of Malacca, vital to trade and communications between the South China Sea and Indian Ocean.

Potential danger

Nor do the problems end there, for if EEZs were to be based on the 1982 proposal of the right of countries to extend their "territorial waters" from 80 to 320 km (50 to 200 miles) from their coastlines, then there are areas in which this would produce a potentially dangerous situation. In the Aegean, for example, many of the small islands are part of Greece and, if the Greeks insist on the right to impose territorial waters, even at 80 km (50 miles), the Turks would be excluded from any mineral exploration or exploitation arrangements. This has, in fact, led to a crisis between the two countries which has gone on for some time. Occasionally, as in March 1987, the

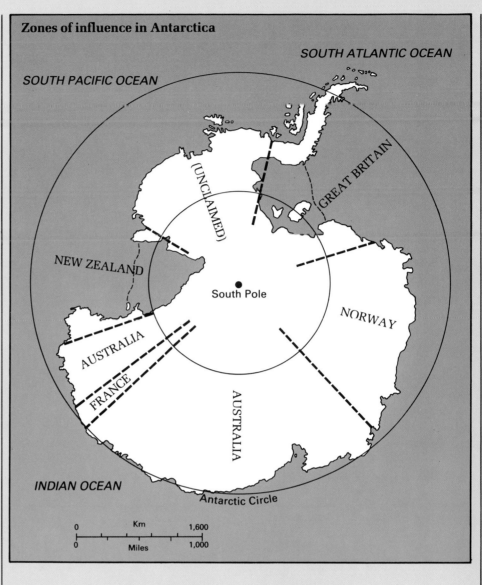

Zones of influence in Antarctica

SOUTH ATLANTIC OCEAN

SOUTH PACIFIC OCEAN

GREAT BRITAIN

(UNCLAIMED)

NEW ZEALAND

South Pole

NORWAY

AUSTRALIA

FRANCE

AUSTRALIA

INDIAN OCEAN

Antarctic Circle

| 0 | Km | 1,600 |
| 0 | Miles | 1,000 |

Turks "test the waters" by sending out exploration vessels, supported by warships – something which the Greeks respond to with threats and naval maneuvers. A crisis is always on the cards, requiring international diplomacy – exercised through the North Atlantic Treaty Organization (NATO), to which both countries belong, or the United Nations.

Similar disputes exist between Norway and the Soviet Union in the Barents Sea; between the Soviet Union and Japan in the Okhotsk Sea; and between Britain and Iceland in the waters of the North Atlantic. The latter led to the so-called "Cod Wars" of the 1970s as Icelandic fishery protection vessels tried to prevent British fishing boats from operating within 320 km (200 miles) of Iceland.

Antarctica

All this makes the sea a potential source of conflict and adds weight to the need for workable international laws. The 1982 Law of the Sea Conference, with its EEZs and extended territorial waters, did little to solve the problems and, with the future of Antarctica in the balance, something more is clearly needed.

At the moment, Antarctica is divided into a number of "zones" of influence, administered by Australia, Britain, Norway, New Zealand and France, but as the mineral resources of the area become more and more vital, other countries are going to demand a share. Both Argentina and Chile have claims in the area. The 1961 Antarctic Treaty did not settle these. In such circumstances, disputes are likely.

MAJOR TERRORIST GROUPS

There are a large number of terrorist groups in the modern world, and a complete checklist would be difficult to compile. The following are the most important, having been responsible for the vast majority of incidents which became headline news during the last 20 years. Their aims – whether nationalist, revolutionary or anarchist – are typical of those pursued by less significant groups.

The PLO

Formed in May 1964, the Palestine Liberation Organization (PLO) has developed into a "government-in-exile" for the Palestinian people, dedicated to the restoration of lands now occupied by Israel. Dominated since February 1969 by Yasser Arafat and his *Fatah* group, the PLO has had an uneven history. Militarily, it has achieved little, having been defeated both in Jordan (1970-71) and in Lebanon (1982), but politically it has significant strength,

not least in the United Nations where, since 1974, it has enjoyed "observer status." Such an emphasis upon diplomacy, however, has led many Palestinians to doubt the effectiveness of the PLO in the struggle against Israel, and a number of "splinter groups" have emerged. These include:

The Popular Front for the Liberation of Palestine (PFLP), formed in November 1967 by George Habash. Responsible for a number of aircraft hijacks and kidnappings in the 1970s, often with the help of terrorists from other, non-Palestinian groups.

The PFLP-General Command, formed in 1969 by Ahmed Jibril and responsible for a number of cross-border attacks into Israel in the 1970s.

The Popular Democratic Front for the Liberation of Palestine (PDFLP), formed in 1969 by Naif Hawatmeh, also responsible for attacks on Israel.

Black September, formed in 1971 to commemorate Palestinian actions in

the war against Jordan (which began in September 1970); responsible for a number of horrific terrorist acts, including the Lod Airport and Munich Olympics massacres (May and September 1972).

Black June, or Abu Nidal Group, formed in 1976 by Sabri al-Banna (Abu Nidal), chiefly in protest at the Syrian intervention in Lebanon against the Palestinians. Responsible for (among others) the incidents at Rome and Vienna airports (December 1985) and the hijack of a Pan American Boeing 747 to Karachi in Pakistan (September 1986).

The Baader-Meinhof Gang/Red Army Faction

Formed in 1970 by Andreas Baader, Ulrike Meinhof and Gudrun Ensslin in West Germany. With roots in the student protests of the late 1960s, the Gang received training from the Palestinians in Jordan before starting a wave of bomb attacks and bank robberies which continued until 1972, when the leaders were all arrested. Despite their subsequent suicides in 1976 and 1977, their actions have been continued by the Red Army Faction, with involvement in various international incidents. Close contacts with the PFLP have now been replaced by contacts with the French terrorist group, *Action Directe*.

The Italian Red Brigades

Formed in 1974 by left-wing activists disillusioned with the Italian Communist Party. The Italian authorities did little to curb their campaign of assassinations and kidnappings until public opinion was outraged by the kidnapping and murder of Aldo Moro, an ex-prime minister and president of the Christian Democrat Party (1978). Since then, the killings and bombings have continued, but with the original leaders arrested and imprisoned, the level of violence has declined.

PLO members leave Lebanon, 1982.

The Red Brigades terrorist convicted of killing Aldo Moro.

The ETA

Formed in 1959, *Euskadi Ta Askatasun* (ETA) is dedicated to achieving independence for the Basque region of northern Spain. Assassinations and murders are the hallmarks of the group – in December 1973, for example, it killed Admiral Carrero Blanco by planting a bomb in his car, and in July 1986 it murdered nine members of the Civil Guard by blowing up the bus in which they were traveling.

The IRA

Formed in 1916 from the Irish Republican Brotherhood, the Irish Republican Army (IRA) has the longest history of terrorism of any group in the Western world. After mounting a successful campaign to oust the British from southern Ireland (1919-21), they were forced underground by the new Dublin government, emerging briefly in 1939 and 1956-63 to attack British targets in Northern Ireland and on the mainland. In 1969, the IRA was caught unprepared by the civil rights troubles in the North and, in the subsequent debates about policy, it split into Official and Provisional wings (1970). Both groups have continued to mount attacks on targets in the North and on the mainland; there is evidence to suggest links in the past with both the Palestinians and Gaddafi of Libya. In more recent years, the impact of the IRA has been diluted by internal splits, one of which produced the Irish National Liberation Army (INLA), a group prepared to use even greater violence to achieve its aims of nationalist revolution.

Hezbollah

Formed in Lebanon in the aftermath of the Israeli invasion (June 1982), the *Hezbollah* (Party of God) is a Shi'ite Muslim group dedicated to the principles of fundamentalist revolution as preached by the Iranian leader, Ayatollah Khomeini. Anti-Israeli and anti-Western, it has been responsible for a number of terrorist incidents in Lebanon, the most shocking of which was the use of truck-bombs against US and French forces in Beirut on October 23, 1983, in which almost 300 soldiers died.

IRA demonstrators barricade a street with a burning truck, 1981.

ANTI-TERRORIST SPECIAL FORCES

As part of their response to the threat of terrorism, many liberal democracies have created elite special units, trained in the anti-terrorist role. Drawn from military, paramilitary and police forces, these units are available to monitor terrorist activities and, in the event of an incident, to mount rescue missions. Not all have succeeded, but the overall record is impressive, showing the determination of the democracies to protect their citizens.

Delta Force (United States of America)

Established in July 1978, the Special Forces Operational Detachment – Delta (known simply as Delta Force) was the brainchild of Colonel Charles Beckwith, a Special Forces officer with combat experience in Vietnam. Basing his ideas firmly on those of Britain's SAS (with whom he had served as an exchange officer in 1962), Beckwith created a highly trained counter-terrorist unit. In April 1980 Delta Force was assigned to rescue members of the US embassy in Tehran, held hostage by Revolutionary Guards, but the operation ended in failure as transport helicopters were lost to accident and adverse desert conditions.

Israeli Paratroopers

Although primarily an elite airborne unit for use in conventional military operations, Israel's parachute forces have a reputation for counter-terrorist work, based upon their successful rescue mission to Entebbe (Uganda) in July 1976. Commanded by Lieutenant-Colonel Netanyahu, 86 paratroopers flew to Entebbe late on July 3, landing secretly and then storming the Old Terminal building to rescue some 96 Israeli citizens, held by members of the Popular Front for the Liberation of Palestine and Baader-Meinhof terrorist groups. Netanyahu was killed in the assault, but otherwise the mission was a complete success.

GSG9 (West Germany)

Formed in 1972 in the aftermath of the Munich Olympics incident, when 11 Israeli athletes were murdered by Palestinian terrorists, Grenzschutzgruppe Neun (GSG9) is not part of the Federal German Army but is drawn from the paramilitary Border Police. Colonel Ulrich Wegener was ordered to create the new unit and, by 1973, he had put together the basics of an 188-man force, specializing in counter-terrorist work. Three or four "strike units," each of 30-42 men, form the spearhead of GSG9, backed by communications, intelligence and engineer specialists. The men of GSG9 became national heroes in October 1977 after their successful storming of a hijacked Lufthansa 737 at Mogadishu (Somalia).

An Israeli officer explains how the paratroopers were able to storm the terminal at Entebbe, 1976.

Delta Force members undergo an arduous training program.

GIGN (France)

The *Groupe d'Intervention Gendarmerie Nationale* (GIGN) was formed in November 1973, soon after the French had failed to deal effectively with a terrorist takeover of the Saudi Arabian embassy in Paris. Drawn from the paramilitary *Gendarmerie Nationale*, the initial GIGN force comprised only 15 men, divided into three five-man teams, but by 1976 the establishment had been increased to two officers and 40 men, organized into "strike teams." In early February 1976, one of these teams, backed by men of the French Foreign Legion, successfully stormed a hijacked schoolbus in Djibouti, taken by terrorists of the Somali Coast Liberation Front. All the terrorists were shot by GIGN snipers after the schoolchildren had been given food laced with drugs to send them to sleep.

GEO (Spain)

The *Grupo Especial de Operaciones* (GEO) was formed in 1978 specifically to operate in an anti-terrorist role. Under the control of the National Police but recruited from the armed forces as a whole, GEO comprises specially selected volunteers who are trained according to patterns and principles laid down by the SAS and GSG9. GEO is organized into three groups of eight "sticks," each of five men. GEO has yet to operate against terrorists but it successfully stormed a bank in Barcelona, in May 1981, when it was taken over by robbers.

Sa'Aqa (Egypt)

Formed in the early 1970s from Egyptian commando forces, *Sa'Aqa* (Lightning) has enjoyed mixed success. Although used to storm a hijacked Boeing 737 at Luxor airport (Egypt) in 1975, it failed to rescue hostages at Larnaca (Cyprus) in March 1978 and operated with only partial success at Luqa (Malta) in November 1985, when 59 of the 98 hijack victims failed to survive a rescue attempt.

SAS (Great Britain)

First formed in North Africa in 1941, the Special Air Service (SAS) Regiment soon gained a reputation for long-range attacks deep behind enemy lines. Disbanded in 1945, it re-emerged in 1952 when the Malayan Scouts, raised to conduct anti-guerrilla operations in the Malayan jungle, were renamed 22 SAS. Since then, the unit has specialized in counterinsurgency, serving in Borneo (1963-66), Aden (1964-67), Northern Ireland (post-1969) and Dhofar (1970-75), but has also resumed its earlier role of long-range reconnaissance and attack, most notably in the Falklands (1982). In 1975 a special Counter-Revolutionary Warfare (CRW) group was added, specifically for anti-terrorist work: it was this group which carried out the highly acclaimed mission to storm the Iranian embassy in London in May 1980, when Arab terrorists from Iran had seized a number of Iranian and British hostages.

UN PEACEKEEPING OPERATIONS

Since 1945, the role of United Nations' forces has been a subject of some controversy. After the experience of Korea (1950-53), when UN troops were committed specifically to fight an aggressor, many countries refused to allow further deployments unless in a non-fighting capacity.

Out of this emerged the idea of "peace-keeping" rather than "peace-making." Success has been mixed and peace-keeping forces can never be expected to solve the problems which lead to war, but their existence can produce calm, allowing more peaceful negotiations to take place.

Suez, 1956-67
After the end of hostilities between Israel, Egypt, the United Kingdom and France in November 1956, United Nations Emergency Force I (UNEF I) occupied the Canal Zone. After the Israeli evacuation of Sinai in March 1957, the force remained in the Gaza Strip for the next 10 years, being withdrawn in May 1967 at the request of President Gamal Abdel Nasser of Egypt, on whose territory it was operating. Nasser was then able to invade Israel.

Lebanon, 1958
In 1958, a 600-member UN observer group was invited in by the Lebanese government to prevent the sending of supplies to Muslim factions from across the Syrian frontier. The United Nations Observer Group in Lebanon (UNOGIL) was restricted to observation and reporting back to the Security Council, and was not allowed to intervene directly. UNOGIL ended at the request of the Lebanese government in December 1958. It was an excellent example of a rapid response, made possible by the availability of a group of experienced personnel in the UN Truce Supervision Organization (UNTSO).

Belgian, Congo, 1960-64
The only time the Secretary-General was authorized to provide military assistance to government forces came in 1960 after the withdrawal of the Belgians from the Congo (Zaire). Until such time as the Congolese government was able to reorganize its forces, the United Nations did its best to maintain the peace, even committing troops to ensure that the province of Katanga (Shaba) did not break away. In the event, the UN force remained for four years and then left. It did not prevent the civil war, but it did prevent the country from breaking up.

West New Guinea (West Irian), 1962
A dispute between the Netherlands and Indonesia over the future of West New Guinea was negotiated peacefully in 1962 by the sending in of UNTEA (UN Temporary Executive Authority), a 1,500-strong military force. UNTEA was a face-saving device which enabled the Dutch to pull out without transferring sovereignty to Indonesia immediately. Within a year the Indonesians had taken over the western part of the island on the understanding that the population would be given an opportunity to vote on whether they wished to remain part of Indonesia.

Yemen, 1962-64
In September 1962 the UN Yemen Observation Mission (UNYOM) was invited in after a civil war following the overthrow of the government. During that year both sides had been backed by Egypt and Saudi Arabia respectively. In an attempt to prevent hostilities from breaking out between those two countries, UNYOM did its best to restrict the scope of the conflict. It was small by the standards of forces sent to the Congo and Suez. But it managed to contribute to a reduction of tension in the region.

Cyprus, 1964-
Initially sent to Cyprus to bring an end to the fighting which broke out between Greek and Turkish factions on the island, the United Nations Force in Cyprus (UNFICYP) was given the role of observing and patrolling certain areas to restore essential government services. The fighting continued nevertheless for the next 10 years. By its intervention, the United Nations might even be said to have provoked conflict at a lower level of violence, from civil strife to street bombings. Like its intervention in Suez (1956-67) it merely served to postpone an inevitable showdown, which occurred in 1974 when Turkey invaded the island on behalf of the Turkish minority. Since 1974, UNFICYP has continued to operate, but only along the "Green Line" dividing Turkish and Greek-Cypriot areas of the island.

Middle East, 1973-79
The Second UN Emergency Force (UNEF II), 7,000-strong, was sent in 1973 to divide the Israeli and Egyptian forces in the Sinai and to supervise a ceasefire. The terms of UNEF II were extended in January 1974 so that it could assist in the disengagement of the two armies. It was further extended from November 1975 to May 1979 to supervise the installation of buffer zones in which neither side was able to hold territory. A separate peace treaty between Egypt and Israel in March 1979 as a result of negotiations conducted under the auspices of the United States led to the termination of UNEF II in July. A peace-keeping force, including forces from Great Britain and Italy, was sent in its place. The latter is not controlled by the United Nations.

A separate UN Disengagement Force has been deployed on the Golan Heights, separating Israel and Syria, since October 1973.

Lebanon, 1978-

On March 11, 1978, the PLO conducted a commando raid on Israel. In retaliation, Israeli forces invaded Lebanon and, in a few days, occupied the entire region south of the Litani River. On the request of the Lebanese government, the Security Council sent a UN interim force (UNIFIL) to restore peace, oversee the withdrawal of Israeli forces and assist the Lebanese government to regain control of the area so that PLO operations could be contained.

The force – 7,000-strong – failed in its task. PLO activities actually increased. By July 1981 over 450 PLO commandos were operating in the UNIFIL area alone, in 30 separate encampments. In June 1982, after another terrorist incident, Israel invaded Lebanon for a second time, pushing the UNIFIL force aside on its way to Beirut in an attempt to destroy the PLO once and for all as a military unit.

UNIFIL is still in place, but occupies an extremely difficult position, being distrusted by all sides in the Lebanon conflict. Various UNIFIL contingents (notably the French and Irish) have lost troops to armed attack.

India/Pakistan 1949, 1965-66

UNMOGIP (the United Nations Military Observer Group in India/Pakistan) had its origins in a conflict between the two countries over the status of Kashmir. A UN India-Pakistan Observation Mission (UNIPOM) was created when conflict occurred in 1947 along the borders outside the UNMOGIP area. With the conclusion of the Karachi agreement in 1949 the situation along the ceasefire line became more stable. Although incidents took place from time to time, they were generally minor. A conflicting claim again in 1965 led to further UN intervention, which was terminated the following year after a separate treaty between the two countries this time negotiated under the auspices of the Soviet Union at Tashkent.

Above: UNMOGIP in Kashmir, 1955. Below: UNIFIL troops in Lebanon, 1978.

CHRONOLOGY-TERRORISM

1968

July 22 PFLP hijack El Al Boeing 707: Israelis agree to terms for the release of hostages

December 26 PFLP grenade-attack on El Al plane, Athens airport (Israelis respond with commando raid on Beirut airport, Lebanon, December 28)

1969

August 29 PFLP hijack TWA Boeing 707: aircraft flown to Damascus (Syria) and destroyed

September 4 Charles Elbrick, US ambassador to Brazil, kidnapped; released after Brazilian government agrees to demands

1970

September 6-12 Dawson's Field (Jordan): three airliners hijacked by PFLP, then blown up

October 5 James Cross, British Trade Commissioner, kidnapped by *Front de Libération de Quebec* (FLQ); released, December 3

October 10 Pierre Laporte, Quebec Minister of Labor, kidnapped by FLQ; murdered, October 18

1972

May 8 Black September hijack Sabena Airlines Boeing 707: flown to Lod (Israel). Israeli commandos storm the plane

May 11 Baader-Meinhof Gang plants bombs in US military installations in West Germany

May 30 Lod Airport massacre: 28 people killed by members of Japanese Red Army (in PFLP pay)

September 5 Munich Olympics: 11 Israeli athletes killed by Black September

1973

March 1 Black September terrorists seize American embassy in Khartoum (Sudan); US ambassador murdered

December 20 Admiral Carrero Blanco assassinated in Madrid by ETA

1974

September 13 Japanese Red Army terrorists seize French embassy in The Hague (Netherlands); first involvement by "Carlos"

November 21 IRA plant bombs in two public houses in Birmingham (England); 19 people killed

1975

December 2 South Moluccan terrorists seize a train at Beilen (Netherlands); surrender, December 11

December 6 IRA gang besieged by British security forces in Balcombe Street (London); surrenders, December 12

December 21 PFLP terrorists (led by "Carlos") seize OPEC oil ministers in Vienna (Austria); released after ransom paid

1976

February 3 French GIGN rescues hijacked schoolchildren in Djibouti (East Africa)

June 27 Air France A300 airliner hijacked by PFLP/Baader-Meinhof group; flown to Entebbe (Uganda)

July 3 Israeli paratroopers storm Entebbe terminal; hostages rescued

August 23 Palestinians hijack Egyptair Boeing 737 and fly to Luxor; plane stormed by *Sa'Aqa*

1977

May 23 South Moluccans seize a train and a primary school in the Netherlands. Both sieges broken by Dutch Marines, June 11

September 5 Red Army Faction kidnaps West German industrialist Hanns-Martin Schleyer; murdered, October 19

October 13 Arab terrorists seize Lufthansa Boeing 737; after various refueling stops (and the death of the pilot), plane lands at Mogadishu (Somalia)

October 18 West German GSG9 commandos storm the hijacked plane at Mogadishu: hostages rescued. Baader-Meinhof leaders commit suicide

1978

March 16 Italian Red Brigades kidnap Aldo Moro; murdered, May 9

1979

August 27 IRA murder Earl Mountbatten at Mullaghmore (Ireland)

November 4 US embassy in Tehran (Iran) seized by Revolutionary Guards

1980

April 24 US rescue mission to Tehran fails

May 5 SAS storms Iranian embassy in London; hostages rescued

August 2 Right-wing terrorists bomb Bologna railway station (Italy): 84 people killed

1983

October 23 Hezbollah terrorists bomb US and French peace-keeping HQs in Beirut (Lebanon); over 300 soldiers killed

1984

October 12 IRA attempt to assassinate British prime minister, Margaret Thatcher, at Grand Hotel, Brighton (England)

1985

June 14 Lebanese terrorists hijack TWA Boeing 727 to Beirut: one US serviceman killed

June 23 Sikh extremists plant a bomb on an Air India airliner: 347 people killed

October 7 Italian cruise liner *Achille Lauro* hijacked: one US citizen killed

November 23 Palestinian terrorists hijack Egyptian jet, killing 2. Egyptian commandos storm plane, killing 57 in rescue attempt

December 27 Abu Nidal Group attacks Rome and Vienna airports: 17 people killed

1986

April 5 Abu Nidal Group plants bomb in La Belle Disco, West Berlin; US serviceman killed

April 14-15 US air raid on Tripoli (Libya) in retaliation for April 5

July 14 Nine Spanish Civil Guards killed by ETA

September 5 Pan American Boeing 747 hijacked to Karachi (Pakistan): 20 hostages killed

September Wave of bombings in Paris (France) in support of imprisoned Lebanese terrorist, Georges Abdallah

CHRONOLOGY-WARS

1945-December 1949 Chinese Civil War (Nationalists versus Communists)

1945-October 1949 Greek Civil War (Royalists versus Communists)

1945-July 1954 First Indochina War (France versus Communists)

May 1948-January 1949 Arab-Israeli War – Israel's War of Independence (Israel versus Egypt, Jordan, Iraq, Syria and Lebanon)

June 1948-July 1960 Malayan Emergency (Britain versus Communists)

June 1950-July 1953 Korea (United Nations versus North Korea and China)

November 1954-March 1962 Algeria (Nationalists versus France)

November 1955-December 1959 Cyprus Emergency (Britain versus Greek-Cypriots)

July-November 1956 Suez Crisis (Britain, France and Israel versus Egypt)

December 1956-January 1959 Cuban Revolt (Government versus Communists)

1957-80 Rhodesia (Zimbabwe) (Government versus Insurgents)

1959-April 1975 Second Indochina War (Vietnam) (South Vietnam versus North Vietnam; United States involved, 1965-73)

July 1960-December 1967 Congo (Zaire) (Government versus Factions)

August 1960- Chad (Government and France versus rebels)

1961-November 1976 Angola (Nationalists versus Portugal and, from November 1975, MPLA versus FNLA and UNITA)

October-November 1962 Sino-Indian War (China versus India)

April 1963-August 1966 Confrontation in Borneo (Malaysia and Britain versus Indonesia)

December 1963-November 1967 Aden (Nationalists versus Britain)

1964-June 1975 Mozambique (Nationalists versus Portugal)

April-September 1965 Indo-Pakistan War (India versus Pakistan)

May 1967-July 1970 Nigerian Civil War (Nigeria versus Biafra)

June 1967 Arab-Israeli "Six-Day" War (Israel versus Egypt, Jordan and Syria)

August 1969- Northern Ireland (Britain versus Republicans)

December 1971 Indo-Pakistan War (India versus Pakistan)

October 1973 Arab-Israeli "Yom Kippur" War (Israel versus Egypt and Syria)

September 1975- Lebanese Civil War (Christian versus Muslim Factions)

1976- Namibia (South Africa versus SWAPO guerrillas)

1978-79 Ogaden War (Ethiopia versus Somalia)

May 1979- Nicaragua (Government versus Sandinista guerrillas and, from July 1979, Sandinistas versus US-backed Contras)

December 1979- Afghanistan (Soviet Union versus *Mujaheddin* guerrillas)

September 1980- Gulf War (Iran versus Iraq)

April-June 1982 Falklands War (Britain versus Argentina)

June 1982 Israeli Invasion of Lebanon (Israel versus PLO, Syria and Muslim Factions)

INDEX

FURTHER READING

Becker, Jillian, *The Rise and Fall of the Palestinian Liberation Organization* (St. Martin's Press, 1984)

Beckwith, Charlie A and Donald Knox, *Delta Force: The Army's Elite Counter-terrorist Unit* (Dell, 1985)

Brandt, Willy and Anthony Sampson, eds., *North-South: A Program for Survival* (The Brandt Report). (MIT Press, 1980)

Carlton, David and Carlo Schaerf, eds., *Contemporary Terror: Studies in Sub-state Violence* (St. Martin's Press, 1981)

Carroll, Raymond, *The Future of the U.N.* (Franklin Watts, 1985)

Caserta, John S, *The Red Brigades* (Woodhill, 1978)

Cobban, Helena, *The Palestinian Liberation Organization: People, Power, Politics* (Cambridge University Press, 1984)

Coogan, Tim, *The I.R.A.* (Fontana, England) (Irish Book Centre, 1971)

Dobson, Christopher and Ronald Payne, *Counterattack: The West's Battle Against the Terrorist* (Facts on File, 1982)

Fanon, Frantz, *The Wretched of the Earth* (Grove, 1965)

Freeman, Charles, *Terrorism in Today's World* (David and Charles, 1980)

Harrison, Paul, *Inside the Third World* (Humanities Press, 1979)

Laqueur, Walter, *Terrorism* (Little, Brown & Co., 1979)

Laqueur, Walter, *The Terrorism Reader: A Historical Anthology* (Temple University Press

Mickolus, Edward, *Transnational terrorism: A Chronology of Events 1968-1979* (Greenwood, 1980)

Netanyahu, Benjamin, ed., *Terrorism: How the West can Win* (Farrar, Straus & Giroux, 1986)

Raynor, Thomas P, *Terrorism: Past, Present, Future,* (rev. ed. Franklin Watts, 1987)

Taheri, Amir, *The Spirit of Allah* (Alder and Alder, 1985)

(Note: All publishers located in New York unless specified otherwise)

ACKNOWLEDGMENTS

Cover: Frank Spooner; contents page: Stern; page 9: Hutchison; page 10: Stern; page 12: Barry Lewis/Network; page 14: Stern; page 16: Stern; page 17: Stern; page 22: Hutchison; page 24: Frank Spooner; page 25: Stern; page 26: Photosource; page 29 (both): Stern; page 30: Frank Spooner; page 33: Network; page 34: Stern; pages 36-37: Frank Spooner; page 38: Topham Picture Library; page 42: John Hillelson; page 44: United Nations, London; page 45: Popperfoto; page 46: Stern; page 48 (all): Popperfoto; page 49 (all): Popperfoto; page 52: The Research House; page 53 (top): Popperfoto; page 53 (bottom): Stern; page 54: Stern; page 55: The Research House; page 57 (top): Stern; page 57 (bottom): United Nations.